# Crazy Faith

## Written by Dr. Linda Smith

RSG Publishing LLC
www.rsgpublishing.com

*NOTE: If you purchased this book without a cover you should be aware that this book is stolen property. It was reported as "unsold and destroyed' to the publisher, and neither the author nor the publisher has received any payment for this "stripped book."*

Printed in the United States of America
Copyright © Linda Smith, 2007.

All rights reserved. No part of this book may be stored or introduced into a retrieval system or transmitted, in any form, or by any means electronic, mechanical, or recording or used or reproduced in any manner whatsoever without written permission except in cases of brief quotations used in articles or reviews. The scanning, uploading, and distribution of this book via the Internet or via any other means without the publisher's permission is illegal and punishable by law. For information regarding permission, write to RSG Publishing LLC, P.O. Box 116, Accokeek MD, 20607

ISBN -13: 978-0-9825735-4-9
ISBN -10: 0-9825735-4-5
Library of Congress Control Number: 2017960307

Published by RSG Publishing, LLC
P.O. Box 116
Accokeek MD 20607
www.rsgpublishing.com

Inside layout by EYES INC. www.eyesinc.org

Scriptures: Scripture taken from King James Open Bible Expanded Edition. Copyright ©1985 by Thomas Nelson. Used by permission. All rights reserved. Scripture taken from The King James Study Bible. Copyright ©1985 by Thomas Nelson. Used by permission. All rights reserved. Scripture references marked MSG are taken from The Message: The Bible in Contemporary Language. Copyright © 2002 by NavPress. All rights reserved. Scripture references marked AMP are taken from The Comparative Study Bible, Amplified Version. Copyright © 1987 by the Zondervan Corporation and the Lockman Foundation. All rights reserved.

# ACKNOWLEDGEMENTS

First and foremost, I want to give all the glory and praise to God, who helped me, pushed me, and prepared me to be able to write this book. My trials, experiences and accomplishments were not only for me but were to help others to know that they can make it, that they can stand during their time of testing.

Next, I want to thank my husband and Pastor, Apostle David Smith, who has always been there for me. You spoke into my life, prayed, encouraged and pushed me to finish this work because you knew it would be a blessing to the body of Christ. Thank you for your love, wisdom and spiritual insight and the gift you bring to the body of Christ by following God's leading in everything that you do. You are truly a wonderful husband and an awesome man of God.

To my sons and their wives - my children: thank you for your love and support of me and this project. You have always stood by me and you've been there through the storms and the rain. Thank you for being the loving family that you are.

Special thanks go to my armor-bearers who spend countless hours fasting and praying for me. I cannot thank you enough for what you do for me on a daily basis. I am grateful that God has chosen you to work closely with me to slay giants in the earth. God will certainly reward you for your labor and faithfulness.

Special thanks also to my cousin (Janet McGill) that labored with me to finish this project. Thank you for knowing how to express my heart in writing, how to hear my words and by them paint a picture in the minds of those who will read this book. God will not forget your labor of love.

# INTRODUCTION

You may ask what is the difference between "Faith" and what I call "Crazy Faith"? Faith comes by hearing and receiving God's Word. Once we receive Jesus by that faith, then He gives us a measure of faith. Crazy faith is a result of growth from "the measure of faith" that God gives to every believer. Crazy faith is literally relying and standing on God's Word regardless of what we see with our eyes. Relying on God's every word will take your faith to another level above your natural senses or consciousness. You will then have hope when hope seemingly cannot be found. The more you rely on God and His Word, the more you know that He will provide. You must believe that God is the same God that you read about in the Bible. He is the same today as He was yesterday, and this allows you to have crazy faith because you believe His Word.

It takes time for faith to develop to maturity. You must go beyond confessing with your mouth and believing in your heart that Jesus is Lord. Spiritual maturity comes by much study and meditation on God's Word coupled with fasting and praying.

It will take crazy faith to keep you functioning in the world in which we live today. The day-to-day struggles, which are nothing more than the devil's distractions, along with current event tragedies, will demand our entire reliance on God as never before!

It took crazy faith to get me spiritually, emotionally, and financially where I am now. And crazy faith can do the same for you! My goal is to help you get past just confessing or speaking words in the air to confessing what God says in His Word regarding our situations and circumstances and actually believing what He says will come to past. We can believe even to the point, if necessary, of forsaking what family, friends, and others have to say. My goal is to help you reach that level of crazy faith!

# 1

## What Is Faith?

There are two types of faith. One is God given faith, and the other is natural faith. Smith Wigglesworth says:

> There is only one way to all the treasures of God, and that is the way of Faith. By faith and faith alone do we enter into a knowledge of the attributes, become partakers of the beatitudes, and participate in the glories of our ascended Lord (Wigglesworth, Faith That Prevails 3).

Our first commitment to faith is salvation. In other words, it takes faith to be saved. Romans 10:9-10 says:

> That if thou shalt confess with thy mouth the Lord Jesus, and shalt believe in thine heart that God hath raised him from the dead, thou shalt be saved. For with the heart man believeth unto righteousness, and with the mouth confession is made unto salvation.

There are two key factors: the mouth and the heart. We must confess with our mouth and believe in our heart. Once you have confessed your faults to the Lord, He has forgiven you and He does not bring the faults up anymore.

> As far as the east is from the west, so far hath He removed our transgressions from us (Psalm 103:12).

What is most tragic is that we have not forgiven ourselves, and therefore we continue to torture ourselves over things the Lord has forgotten. That's why it is hard for you to believe that you're saved. The enemy knows that you're doubtful and that you're asking yourself, "Am I really saved?"

I want you to know that when fear and doubt are evident the enemy will try to tell you you're not saved! Thus, the devil plants a seed in your mind, and you water it. You must know that when you confess with your mouth and believe in your heart that you are saved. No devil in hell can change that. You cannot help if the thought comes to your mind, but don't dwell on it. When you dwell on it, that's when the thought takes root! You must stand firm and say to the devil with power, "I am saved!"

Now that you have confessed with your mouth and believed with your heart, faith is settling in. You can say that you're saved with boldness because you have believed it and confessed it! We must allow ourselves to have the confidence (faith or trust) to know that after we have confessed and believed without doubting, we are saved.

Hebrews 11:1 says, "Now faith is the substance of things hoped for, the evidence of things not seen." But what is that verse truly saying? I like the way Kenneth Hagin put it, "Bible faith is laying hold of the unseen realm of hope and bringing it into the realm of reality."

It is trusting God for whatever you need even though you

cannot see it in front of you. What good is it to say you believe God if you have already made preparation for the things you want or need? I don't have to trust God for something I already have. It is what I don't have that I'm trusting God for!

To have faith is to be firmly persuaded that God will do what He said, and for that which you are expecting, will come to pass. In the "expectation" of what you are hoping for, you'll carry on your daily activities as if the thing has come to pass or "know" that surely this thing shall be brought to reality.

The moment that the request is made, we are to believe as though we have the answer. Mark 11:24 says, "Therefore I say unto you, what things soever ye desire, when ye pray, believe that ye receive them, and ye shall have them".

The "believe" comes before the "receive". If we are praying according to God's will, we know that He hears us:

> And this is the confidence that we have in Him, that, if we ask anything according to His Will, He heareth us:
> And if we know that He hear us, whatsoever we ask, we know that we have the petitions that we desired of Him (I John 5:14-15).

Matthew Henry wrote:

> Faith and hope go together. The same things that are the object of our hope are the object of our faith! Faith is a firm persuasion and expectation that God will perform all that He has promised to you in Christ. This persuasion is so strong that it will give your soul a kind of "possession" of those things.

> Faith demonstrates to the eye of the mind the reality of those things that cannot be discerned by the eye of the body. Faith is designed to serve the believer instead of sight, and to be the soul of all that the senses are to the body. (The NIV Matthew Henry Commentary in One Volume, 736)

Webster describes faith as 1: unquestioning belief that does not require proof or evidence, 2: unquestioning belief in God, religious tenets, 3: complete trust, confidence or reliance. The Layman's Bible Dictionary defines faith as, "Belief and confidence in the testimony of another, particularly God's promise of salvation and eternal life for all who place their trust in Jesus Christ" as in John 5:24:

> Verily, verily, I say unto you, He that heareth my word, and believeth on him that sent me, hath everlasting life, and shall not come into condemnation; but is passed from death unto life.

A gift of "God faith" is essential to salvation, as in Ephesians 2:8, "For by grace are ye saved through faith; and that not of yourselves: *it is* the gift of God." Trust defined is "to put one's confidence in a person or thing." God's name and His Word are worthy of our trust.

If you want to please God you must have faith in Him. Without it you cannot please him no matter how hard you try. (Hebrews 11:6)

Faith is as simple as this: It is believing God without wavering, without doubting and without questioning what He says. It is taking God at His Word and believing that what He has promised will be done. I know that He is able. It is the quality of counting "those things which be not as though they were" (Romans 4:17). Faith is also the absolute certainty that what God has promised and what we have asked according to His Word is *already* done.

Expect the complete answer whether you see it at once or not! Drop your emotions. Forget impossibilities or anything to the contrary, and believe that it shall be done regardless of how impossible it may appear outwardly. Faith laughs at impossibilities and cries out, "IT IS DONE"! It leaves all results and all answers with God as being God's responsibility, and it assumes that it is done.

I remember when my youngest son was playing outside and was struck in the eye by a tree branch. That night I was attending a class and received a call that my son's eyes were rolling in the back of his head. I rushed home and took him to the emergency room. At that moment, I realized that I could pray and believe all day for everyone else's healing, but when my son was hurt that day, I feared that God would not answer my prayer. It is funny how we have enough faith for others, but when it comes to us or our family members, we develop a hiccup in streaming faith.

Well, the doctor told me that my son had scratched his cornea and that he would have to see a specialist the next day. We went home, and I told my husband what the doctor said. I asked him why is it that we can believe God for everyone else, but not for our own child? Not responding, my husband proceeded to pray for our son.

After he prayed, the Lord gave him specific instructions. I really cannot say exactly what God told him, but I do know that God let my husband know that if He can use him to pray for others, why not his own son? He followed the Lord's instructions. When I took our son to the specialist there was not a trace of a scratch or any evidence that something had happened to his eye! God is awesome! He is a Healer! This took my husband's and my faith up another level to that crazy faith that we will believe God for anything.

It takes crazy faith to believe God and not the doctor's report! We put our confidence in God and in what He can do, not in the doctor's ability or our own. Faith is believing that with God the impossibilities of life become possibilities!

# 2

## Protecting Your Faith

Norvel Hayes, the author of <u>How To Protect Your Faith</u>, says, "Faith brings God's power for whatever you need

- into your life
- into your body
- into your business
- into your mind
- into your spirit
- into your children

Your faith will bring His blessing to you for whatever you are believing God to do for you."

Believe God for the impossible! Impossible means you don't see how it can be done. However, Hebrews 11:6 says, "But without faith it is impossible to please Him: for he that cometh to God must believe that He is, and that He is a rewarder of them that diligently seek Him". Therefore, you must believe that God can and that He will!

If we had the kind of faith like Moses, when crossing our Red Seas, we would get something accomplished in God. We are so easy to waiver; then our faith will not go beyond what we cannot naturally control. As long as we have some type of control over our situation and can have some input, only then will we give it to God. We need to put our faith to the test, release complete control of the situation, and believe that God can!

It makes a difference how we deal with trials. We must learn to go through our trials with joy. We must praise God for the good and for the bad. You say, "How can I praise God when I'm going through?" The same way you praise Him when He made a way for you to get that house, car, and whatever else you needed, is the way you praise Him during the bad times. In the book of James, 1:2-4 it says:

> My brethren, count it all joy when ye fall into divers temptations;
> Knowing this, that the trying of your faith worketh patience.
> But let patience have *her* perfect work, that ye may be perfect and entire, wanting nothing.

Another point when we go through trials or tests is, we should not always let others know what we are going through. Put a smile on your face and be like the Shunammite woman and say, "**It Is Well**". (II Kings 4:18-37).

You must understand that God is not going to burden you with problems that you cannot withstand. I Corinthians 10:13 says, "God is faithful, who will not suffer you to be tempted above that ye are able; but will with the temptation also make a way to escape, that ye may be able to bear it."

So, since we know that God is not going to put any more on us than we are able to handle then we must say, "I can handle this through Christ, who strengthens me." Also, we must praise God at all times. We must live the words of Psalms 146:1-6:

> Praise ye the LORD. Praise the LORD, O my soul.
> While I live will I praise the LORD: I will sing praises unto my God while I have any being.
> Put not your trust in princes, nor in the son of man, in whom there is no help.
> His breath goeth forth, he returneth to his earth; in that very day his thoughts perish.
> Happy is he that hath the God of Jacob for his help, whose hope *is* in the LORD his God:
> Which made heaven, and earth, the sea, and all that therein is: which keepeth truth forever...

We all must learn to put our trust in God. Man will fail you, but God will not! Trust me! I know from my life experiences. I can remember when I first got saved, I was looking at people rather than God, and as I was praying, God let me know that I should put my trust in Him. He gave me the scripture, Psalm 118:8. It says, "It is better to trust in the LORD than to put confidence in man." If I had not paid attention to what the Lord had said I would have failed God as some of the people that I looked up to had done.

The next point: We all need to develop patience in our lives. We are so used to the fast paced life of instant gratification. We don't want to wait or go through any kind of process. But God must process, refine us so that He can use us. Refine means to "free from impurities or defects; make or become more, polished, elegant, or cultured." (<u>Oxford Pocket Dictionary and Thesaurus</u> 669).

To me, this means we cannot have any blemishes. We need

to be pure in our thoughts and pure in our walk. We must be washed with the word of God.

Many people feel because they were taught that Jesus loves them that it is okay to live any kind of way. I'm here to tell you that it is not true. You must be born again, as found in John 3:3.

My father is my Protector. He is my guide. He leads me all the way if I allow Him. He also protects me from danger and from fiery darts if I put my trust in Him. Let's look at Psalms 23:1-6:

> The LORD *is* my shepherd; I shall not want.
> He maketh me to lie down in green pastures: he leadeth me beside the still waters.
> He restoreth my soul: he leadeth me in the paths of righteous-ness for his name's sake.
> Yea, though I walk through the valley of the shadow of death, I will fear no evil: for thou art with me; thy rod and thy staff they comfort me.
> Thou preparest a table before me in the presence of mine enemies: thou anointest my head with oil; my cup runneth over.
> Surely goodness and mercy shall follow me all the days of my life: and I will dwell in the house of the LORD forever.

I truly love this scripture because when I think about green pastures. I envision a sea of green grass scattered with dandelions. I see light winds rushing through the grass, and I can feel a sense of peacefulness. If I know Him as my Protector and my Shepherd, then I will trust Him. I must hold onto that and not waiver. I must cultivate that and rest in Him.

The Word of God is your shield of faith. Read it, meditate on it, protect it, and believe it!

# 3

# Taking God at His Word When Others Think You Are Crazy

Do we really believe God is who He says He is? Do we really believe the scripture that says, "Jesus Christ, the same yesterday and today, and forever," (Hebrews 13:8) or Malachi 3:6 that says, "For I am the Lord, I change not; therefore ye sons of Jacob are not consumed." If we say "yes" to those statements, then why do we challenge the faith of other believers? If God is not a man who would lie, and if He does not change, why can't we take Him at His Word?

I remember when the Lord first began to deal with my husband regarding angels. Now, I know I'm about to be challenged, called crazy or something much worse, but I do believe that God still uses angels today. Hebrews 13:2 says, "Be not forgetful to entertain strangers: for thereby some have entertained angels unawares." Now, if that was not made for us today, God would not have inspired someone to write it!

There would be times when God would allow an angel to visit our church services. Some that were in attendance have seen them and tried to describe them. Not only would they visit a church service, they would visit us during prayer. Those that say they see him would normally pass out or collapse under the anointing of God.

I believe we had these visitations because God wanted to take our faith to another realm. The ministry is ordained by God, but sometimes, because of unbelief, God does things to prove Himself.

God would sometimes make us aware of a coming visitation. We would prepare ourselves with fasting and praying. Amos 3:7 says, "Surely the Lord GOD will do nothing, but he revealeth his secret unto his servants the prophets."

And **yes,** I do believe that God is still using Prophets and Apostles today! Those services would be awesome to see! Pastor Smith would pray for everyone in the building unless they refused prayer. God's glory would be seen. No one would be able to stand visited by the power of God. Pastor Smith told us when he laid hands on us that the angel would lay on his hands, too.

Once there was a man who was in attendance and was covered with tattoos. We cannot judge by appearances, but he was not very receptive to anything that was said. Unbelief could be seen in his facial expressions and his body language. Even though he was not very receptive, he allowed Pastor Smith to pray for him. When Pastor Smith prayed, this young man's knees buckled. His face turned red, and you could see that what he was feeling was the awesome presence of God! His expression changed. He opened up his heart and spirit, and God performed "open heart" surgery right before our eyes! He was changed by that experience. We give God glory and the highest praise for what He had done. That was the greatest miracle of all – someone's life was changed by the power of God.

# Dr. Linda Smith

We must believe that God is and we must believe what He has said in His word. God does not and has not changed. What He did yesterday, He can do today if we simply take Him at His Word! Yes, we have been mocked and ridiculed, but none of these things move us. Some have even said that we were a cursed ministry. I have never seen blessings bestowed upon a ministry that was cursed. Most important, I've never seen souls saved, bodies healed, cancers dried up or the lame walk in cursed ministries. All these things take place because we dare to believe God. And God's Word doesn't fail:

> So shall my word be that goeth forth out of my mouth: it shall not return unto me void, but it shall accomplish that which I please, and it shall prosper in the thing whereto I sent it (Isaiah 55:11).

# 4

## Faith to Loose the Shackles

Silas, also known as Silvanus, was a laborer in the gospel along with Paul during his second missionary journey. He was a Roman citizen held in high reputation of the church at Jerusalem. He also was one of the men chosen to accompany Paul and Barnabas to bring the Word to the churches in Antioch, Syria, and Cilicia.

There was a disagreement between Barnabas and Paul, so they decided to separate. Paul and Silas continued on the journey, and Barnabas, choosing another partner, sailed in another direction. As Paul and Silas continued on the journey, the Lord used them to bring many souls to Christ, and many miracles took place.

During their stay, they came upon a young lady who was possessed by a spirit of divination. She was set free by the power of God when Paul commanded the evil spirit to come out of her. Her masters became very angry when this happened because they used her "fortune telling" to make money. Because of this, they caught Paul and Silas, brought them into the marketplace before the magistrates, and accused them of "troubling" the city. The magistrates tore off Paul's and Silas' clothes, beat them severely, and threw them in prison.

This treatment would have been enough to discourage anyone, but because of Paul's and Silas' **faith**, **trust**, and **love** for their Lord and Savior, they did not complain. Instead they gave glory to God!

What happened next is probably one of the most memorable encounters written in the scriptures. The Bible says in Acts 16:26:

> And suddenly there was a great earthquake, so that the foundations of the prison were shaken: and immediately all the doors were opened, and everyone's bands were loosed.

Every believer should take note of this. Deliverance from a desperate situation came **after** Paul and Silas gave glory to God! How many times have we been in desperate situations, and we murmured and complained? Deliverance did not come any sooner when we pouted and asked God, "Why?"

When the enemy came against Judah, Jehoshaphat prayed and appointed singers that went before the army to praise the name of the Lord. When they arrived at the battlefield, the enemy was already dead! Judah defeated their enemy with a praise! (See II Chronicles 20).

The children of Israel conquered Jericho with a praise. God gave them specific instructions to march around Jericho for six days without making a sound. On the seventh day they were told to shout. The trumpets blew, the people shouted "a great shout," and the walls fell! They took the city with a shout! Take your city with a shout! Take what God has promised you with a praise! If we'll only give God praise, shackles will fall off of our lives, and deliverance will come.

Salvation even came to the jailer when he came in to survey

the damage of the earthquake and to kill himself because he thought the prisoners had escaped. When he realized what God had done, he was ready to surrender his life to the Lord. (Acts 16:30). That's the kind of faith we should have – faith to be set free and faith to set someone else free! No matter what Paul and Silas endured, it was not enough to discourage their trust in God.

There have been times of bondage in all of our lives. Sometimes we feel trapped or shackled by the pressures of life but we've got to take God at His Word. I'm not saying that we should be oblivious to what's going on around us, but when things happen that seem to "rock our world", then we must fall on our knees. God wants us to cast every care on Him because He cares for us. When we feel our strength is insufficient, we must rely on Him to carry us. We must release every burden and every care to Him. We must realize, if God did not think we could handle the things that happen in our lives, He would not allow them to happen. He knows that as long as He is on the throne of our heart, we are able to take what the enemy is dishing out. We fail when we try to tackle problems without Him, without His direction and without His care.

God has equipped us with enough faith to be set free from all that ails us or has made provision in His word for our deliverance. Not only can we be delivered, but, with faith, there is enough power to set others free. Our lives should be a testimony to those who do not know Christ. Our reflection of Christ should be enough to set the world free.

# 5

## Walking On Water

I have heard people say, "You need to step out on faith." What does "step out on faith" mean? It means no matter what the circumstances are and what the situations dictate, no matter what's going on in my life right now, I choose to believe God.

Some years ago, I did not have reliable transportation, but I knew God would provide. We were driving a car that was eleven years old and was breaking down all the time. My husband was preaching the Word of God out of town every Sunday, and we had our two small children traveling with us. At that time, I did not know that I could depend on the Word of God for my needs. We were tithers and were faithful in giving; I remembered Malachi 3:10 which says, "…and prove me now herewith, saith the Lord of hosts, if I will not open you the windows of heaven, and pour you out a blessing, that there shall not be room enough to receive it." And I surely did need a blessing in a hurry!

We were in revival at the church that we attended. My husband had not begun pastoring yet. I was looking through a publication called <u>The Bible Truth</u> that our Pastor, the late E.C. Cannon had written for the month. The publication was similar to <u>Our Daily Bread</u>. <u>The Bible Truth</u> contained daily scriptures, words of wisdom, and whatever God would lay on his heart to write. Sometimes we would get the book and lay it aside. But I'm thankful for this particular day that I was reading because if I had not picked the book up that day, I could have missed out on a blessing. In <u>The Bible Truth</u> for that week, it said to believe God for what you wanted. Most of us did a lot of faith talking but never really believed and trusted God. While in service that night our Pastor said that we had two days left to go get what we wanted from God. He put emphasis on houses, cars, and any other material things that was **needed**. He also told us to make sure we spoke to the owner of the business or person in charge where we were to "get what we needed." I knew we needed a car. We had put a lot of miles on the one that we had. It was a 1974 Pinto. Sometimes it would break down, and we would have to pull over on the side of the road and call someone to pick us up. We had been dealing with some difficult times in our finances because my husband had gotten sick and lost his job. Our credit was really shaky. It was so shaky that it would not hold anything! But I stepped out on 'Crazy Faith' and went to a car dealership. I had to get my husband's cousin to take me to the dealership because our car had just had another relapse. On the way to the dealership, I reminded myself to only talk to the owner or the person in charge. When we arrived, a salesperson greeted us (as they normally do), and I asked to speak to the owner. He proceeded to tell me that the owner was out of town and would not be back for two weeks. I told the salesman that I would be back when the owner got back into town. A couple of weeks later I went back to the same dealership, and I asked to speak with the owner. When I met him, I told him that my daddy (God) told me to come and get my car. I know he looked at me like I was crazy, on something, or from another world. I acknowledged that my credit was bad and that I did not have any money. Well, he went through the normal procedures of checking me out. I had to fill out a credit application, and when he got the results, it was as bad as I said it was. He came back into the office and told me that the banks had turned me down. It did not matter that I had financed a car from a company before. Everyone turned me down, and it **looked bad,** but I stood on what the Word said. We always quoted the scripture that God will supply all our needs (Philippians 4:19). Well, my needs were not met because we needed a car to continue to do God's work. <u>The Bible Truth</u> also said to get what I wanted. I knew that a man wrote the book, but **God** inspired him to write it. We were living right, and we were doing the work of the Lord. We were getting tired of going to church and on the way there or back home having to call someone to come and get us.

I told the owner that I could not leave without my car. Before I left the dealership the owner told me that he admired me for what I stood for, and since no one else would stand for the loan **he would**! <u>Look at the favor of God</u>. I've never heard of this before, what about you? When everyone else said no, God touched the owner's heart to say, "Yes!" He told me he believed in me and that if the payment was paid on time every month, it would be easy for me to get another car whenever I needed it. God opened the door, and I jumped out. I followed his directions to the letter. If you do what God tells you, He will work for you. It is not very often that you get an owner of a dealership to sign for you, especially if they do not know you. However, God can touch a person's heart. God knew that my husband was preaching His Word, and we were doing all that we knew to do for Him. We should have never been driving a broken-down car in the first place because we belonged to God, having a royal priesthood. My Father, God, is rich, and He can handle what man cannot. He can open doors and windows that we cannot open on our own, but we must obey and trust Him without doubting. If I had doubted and been disobedient to His Word, we would have never received that blessing. What a mighty God we serve!

When I told my husband that I was going to get a car, he did not want to go along with me because he knew our credit was bad. He knew with the type of credit we had, he would be embarrassed and rejected. He did not have the same level of faith that he now has. When I drove the car into the driveway and blew the horn, he wanted to know whose car I was driving. I said, "Just get in." Since then, I have purchased several brand-new cars from this dealership. Just look at what my God can and will do when we trust Him and take Him at His Word! Gloria Copeland said,

> ...we limit our experience of God's goodness when we fail to listen to and obey His voice as the Jewish people did in Jeremiah's day. We also limit His goodness in our lives by our lack of understanding and our lack of faith...God is absolutely unlimited in His ability and His resources. And He is unlimited in His desire to pour out those resources upon us. We know of nothing that delights Him more than the opportunity to give blessings to His obedient children from His abundance (Copeland, Gloria <u>Blessed Beyond Measure</u> 53, 55).

# 6

## Cannot See A Way

Have you ever had to rely on God for everything? Have you ever had to sell some of your possessions to make ends meet? Have you ever wanted God to open a door and give you what you wanted? If you haven't, I sure have.

In 1987, our former Pastor, the late E.C. Cannon, sent us from Rock Hill, South Carolina to Kannapolis, North Carolina to help him start a ministry there. Well, after two weeks of revival, we were told it was in our hands. That meant every bill that had been made during that two-week period belonged to me and my husband! We knew God was leading us in another area for ministry, but we surely did not know we would be "thrown" into it!

This "event" took some crazy faith not to just say, "Forget it! I'm going back home!" For the next three years, we received no support from the headquarters church. All expenses were dumped in our laps for us to take care of. There was no prior warning of what we would have to endure to start a new ministry. I felt like we were thrown in an ocean, and we had to learn to swim or drown. But there was no way that we would go under because we knew God had called my husband to do HIS work.

## Crazy Faith

It took crazy faith not to become bitter, but it was my duty to stand by my husband and obey God. We did not have any members and had no idea where they would come from. Nevertheless, we knew that God had placed ministry in my husband's heart, and it was going to come to pass. For a long time, we did not have any visitors, and a lady across the street from the church would always tell us to be encouraged and that God would send the people.

With God's leading, and after speaking with Pastor Cannon and receiving his blessing, in January 1990, we left the E.C. Cannon Crusade Ministry and started a ministry of our own. My husband, who was the Pastor, our two sons, and I opened the church. We had church on Saturday night, Sunday morning, and Sunday night. The people would come to our church on Saturday and Sunday night when their church was closed. God touched those in attendance to bless the ministry so that the work could go on, but it was not enough to pay all the bills. Thank God that both of us were working at that time, and we could contribute to the finances of the church along with taking care of our own personal bills. It was a challenge, but we made it. If you are faithful to God, He will bless you more than you can imagine.

Not long after that, the membership grew from four (my family) to nine. We were so happy that God blessed us with these members, and their souls were fed richly with the Word of God. Not only were we standing in faith for the bills to be paid, but for members, too. God did it all!

I can remember the Christmas our precious little membership had raised some funds because they wanted to give us something for the holidays. I was glad to have the money. Then the Lord told my husband to put it **all** back into the ministry. My husband was obedient to God without any hesitation. Could we use the money? **YES! YES!** But we had to obey the Lord. I did not ask any questions. Whatever God said, that's what we did. But in my heart, I knew we could have used that money!

As the New Year was approaching, others began to come to the night services. Then God started touching the hearts of the people to join the church. We had members from Gastonia, Charlotte, Kannapolis, Landis, and from all over the nearby cities. God was blessing the ministry. I did not always understand God's leading, but I stood by the man of God and what the Lord told him to do. Because we did everything God told us to do, He blessed our little church until it was overflowing! I do not know how we got all those people in that little church! It would seat fifty or sixty comfortably. But we would have a crowd of sixty to one hundred! We needed something bigger.

One of the deacons heard that a church on Lane Street in Kannapolis was for sale, looked into it, and brought the information back to the pastor. Our little church pulled together, sold dinners, and got the money for the down payment on the church. The bankers were stunned. They could not believe that we raised that money in such a short time. They did not know who was on our side.

March 13, 1994, our new sanctuary was dedicated. Our motto was then (and still is), "For we walk by faith, not by sight," (II Corinthians 5:7). We cannot always see God's hand. Chuck and Sharon Betters wrote, "…faith is believing God even when we can neither see nor understand Him" (Betters, Chuck and Sharon, Treasures of Faith 21).

In the beginning of the ministry, as I said, I did not always understand God's leading. I did not question His instructions, but I humbled myself and obeyed. Hebrews 10:38 says, "Now the just shall live by faith…"

It is not always easy to simply put your needs or feelings

aside and obey God, but as we grow and our relationship with Him matures, our confidence level grows, our faith matures. We know He did not fail us when we first put our confidence in Him and took Him at His Word. And, over time, seeing God move for us, bring back to life dead situations, fight for us against the enemy, and love us back to Himself when we've faltered and blundered, we know that there is none like our God. He will do and can do just what He said.

It is good to point out that "faith is not a guarantee of a comfortable, stress-free life" nor is it "a way of twisting God's arm" to get what we want from Him. The Betters remind us that Hebrews 11 shows us that sometimes our walk is difficult, and men and women of faith were tortured and died for what they believed. They write:

> When we suffer for the faith we are following the journey of Jesus, the perfect model of faith. Jesus "endured the cross despising the shame" for our sakes. We have no reason to expect anything different…just having faith does not insulate us from sickness, pain, sorrow, and death (Ibid.16).

Though I did not totally understand everything in the early stages of the ministry that God had entrusted to my husband, I can look back and see why God did some things the way He did. Notice, I said, <u>some</u> things, not <u>all things</u>! But as the songwriter put it, I believe, "We'll understand it better by and by!"

Prior to us opening the church it was prophesied that God was going to bless us with a house. We sure did need something of our own because we were paying rent. God did not say when, where, or how, but that we were going to get a house. Mind you, we were still traveling back and forth to church, which was about 50 to 60 miles from where we lived. I started looking for houses, and every house that I looked at my husband was not interested. Therefore, this became a long process. I went to look at about fifteen different houses, and my beloved did not like any of them. Finally, he saw a house he wanted. By this time I was tired of looking at houses and decided if he liked this one, so do I.

We were limited with our funds at that time and did not have any money in our savings account. We went through a realtor, filled out the necessary paperwork, and gave the bank our deposit of one hundred dollars. At that time, one hundred dollars was a lot of money to us. In fact, we could not afford to lose that money.

## It Is A Matter of Timing

Guess what? The bankers turned us down due to our credit history. We lost the money and still had no house. It was tough, but how many of you know that timing is everything?

> To every thing there is a season, and a time to every purpose under the heaven:
> A time to be born, and a time to die; a time to plant, and a time to pluck up that which is planted;
> A time to kill, and a time to heal; a time to break down, and a time to build up; A time to weep, and a time to laugh; a time to mourn, and a time to dance;
> A time to cast away stones, and a time to gather stones together; a time to embrace, and a time to refrain from embracing;
> A time to get, and a time to lose; a time to keep, and a time to cast away;

A time to rend, and a time to sew; a time to keep silence, and a time to speak;
A time to love, and a time to hate; a time of war, and a time of peace (Ecclesiastes 3: 1-8).

The realtor told us that it was not over, especially after we had told him that my husband was a veteran. The realtor told us to sit down and write a letter explaining why our credit was the way it was. I proceeded writing this letter explaining in full detail the circumstances of how we used to have good credit and what had transpired and why our credit was in the shape it was. We also sent the check stubs showing that both of us held full time jobs. Timing is everything. The realtor that we had took the letter to another realtor who read it and said that he was going to take it to the Veteran's Administration personally and that we should hear something within the week. Well, we knew what happened the last time, so we did not get excited about this. We did not want to be blown away by the "No"! Just as the realtor promised, we had an answer by the end of the week. I need to mention that before we gave the man the letter with the application, we prayed over the letter and application that God's Will would be done. When the realtor called us at the end of the week, he told us that our application had been accepted. We were happy! It took six weeks for the banks here in town to say "No," and it only took the Veteran's Administration one week to tell us "yes!" Look how God works! I told you it was all in timing. Once we were approved, it was time to talk about money. You will never believe what God did. He touched the hearts of many people because all we had to do was put down five hundred dollars on a ninety-two-thousand dollar house! We did not have to pay closing costs because the owner paid it!

Sometimes we look at our struggles while we are going through them and get sad, but we really don't know what the victory is until the end. God is so great. We have been living in the same house now for sixteen years, and the value of the house has gone up. It took six years for the prophecy of the house to come to pass; nevertheless, it did come to pass. We give God the praise and the glory for what He had done. There is no way we could have what we have if God had said no.

I love the Lord with all my heart and have no other desire but to serve Him until the day I die. This is not because of what He has done but because HE is worthy of the praise and the honor, and I can never stop thanking Him for all He has done for my family and me.

# 7

## Faith in God Is Real

God's word is real, and it must be real to you. In order to know that it is real to you, you must have an intimate relationship with the Lord. This means you must study the Word of God. II Timothy 2:15 says, "Study to show thyself approved unto God, a workman that needeth not to be ashamed, rightly dividing the word of truth." It is more than just reading the Bible.

If we study and obey the word of God, that allows our way to be prosperous and have good success (Joshua 1:8). Most of us don't have the faith to catch onto Joshua 1:8 because we look to man to define success. God can give us great success if we trust and never doubt Him.

The Word has to come alive to you. It cannot be just words on the pages of a book. If you take the Word and eat it as though you were enjoying your favorite food, if you allow your food to digest, you will be surprised at the outcome of your growth. This is something I had to learn for myself - to eat the Word of God. We always say we have faith in God, but we don't yet believe His Word. If we believed His Word, some of the storms, roadblocks, and mountains we face would be dissolved.

## CRAZY FAITH

We all have read Hebrews 11:1 that says, "Now faith is the substance of things hoped for, the evidence of things not seen." "Now faith" means right now, present tense.

Hebrews 11:6 says we must have faith in order to please God. We will not go out of our way to please God, but we will go out of our way to please men. In the natural, the human side of us, we want the praises of men. We will work over-time to get the job done or to please our employer, but we will not stay in the Word of God until we get an understanding. If our employer says, "I want this right now," some of us will do whatever it takes to get it done. I worked on a job where it was my responsibility to get the work done, regardless of the work load that I had, and if I could not, they would find someone who could. It is amazing what we will do for our employers, because they are the source of our pay. We, as Christians, must realize who our real source of our spiritual life is, and that's the Lord. We should know that the pay that comes from God is far greater than any pay check from man. You see, with God, you have your life, health, and strength which no man can give you. Think of the air that you breathe. It comes from God. How many of us know that God **can** and God **will** take care of us, if we allow Him? The Bible says that God will supply all our needs (Philippians 4:19). Because God is alive in me, I know that He will take care of all my needs, and I will desire to do His will. If you do not know what His will is, it is up to you to get your Bible out and start reading the Word. When you know what His will is, then your faith will increase, and your faith will increase to levels that had seemed unattainable before.

I mentioned becoming intimate with the Lord. Reading God's Word does bring intimacy, but it should also be coupled with prayer. The study of God's Word and prayer go hand-in-hand. As we study God's Word, we know what to pray and how to pray, and our Faith will be strengthened. Hebrews 11:6 also mentions, "...He is a rewarder of them that diligently seek Him."

## Dr. Linda Smith

If we ask, it will be given; if we seek, we will find; if we knock, it shall be opened to us. (Matthew 7:7-8) Faith is cultivated in prayer. It becomes real. The more time we spend praying God's Word and seeing the results of our prayers, the more real faith becomes.

> This book of the law shall not depart out of thy mouth; but thou shalt meditate therein day and night, that thou mayest observe to do according to all that is written therein: for then thou shalt make thy way prosperous, and then thou shalt have good success (Joshua 1:8).

# 8

## Crazy Faith at the Red Sea

The Israelites needed to have crazy faith to follow Moses into the desert. It was the lack of this faith that must have caused the murmuring and complaining. However, the people of God had witnessed His power in the land of Egypt. Now they found themselves trapped between Pharaoh's army and the Red Sea. Was it a light thing that the pillar of cloud followed them by day and a pillar of fire by night? If not, why did they begin to complain again and wished they had stayed in Egypt? It was in God's plan to lure Pharaoh into the desert and make him think the children of Israel were trapped with no way of escape. Again, God showed Himself marvelous and told Moses to stretch his rod over the sea, and the sea became dry land.

Can you imagine, walls of water standing up while you walk through on dry ground? I believe their faith was being tested. The Israelites had to trust Moses, the man of God, and follow his instructions. Their faith had to take them across the sea. In my mind, I see a wall of water. Not a drop of water fell. There were no leaks. When God does something, it is done right, from the beginning to the end. If this miracle were to happen today, we would have some skeptics, some doubters in the group who would make others doubt what they were seeing. For example, when God has done something for you and you know that it was God that did it, someone will try to tell you that it was your own hard work and "luck" that got you what you wanted and where you are. Why is it that you will start believing that lie and forget that God's Word says that He is a rewarder of them that diligently seek Him?

When Pharaoh and his army approached, the Israelites became fearful because they were unarmed and seemingly trapped. The people cried out to the Lord and complained to Moses. This cry was a cry of fear, doubt, and unbelief. They lacked the faith they needed to stand up against Pharaoh until Moses said… "Fear ye not, stand still, and see the salvation of the Lord." (Exodus 14:13) The enemy wants us to fear so that doubt and unbelief can creep in and make us lose out with God. But the Word of God says that God looked down through the pillar of fire and of the cloud. The Egyptians were pursuing the children of Israel, but God "discomfited" them or threw them into confusion. For God had promised, "…for the Egyptians whom ye have seen today, ye shall see them again no more for ever." (Exodus 14:13) Let's see what happened:

> And the LORD said unto Moses, Stretch out thine hand over the sea, that the waters may come again upon the Egyptians, upon their chariots, and upon their horsemen.
> And Moses stretched forth his hand over the sea, and the sea returned to his strength when the morning appeared; and the Egyptians fled against it; and the LORD overthrew the Egyptians in the midst of the sea.
> And the waters returned, and covered the chariots, and the horsemen, and all the host of Pharaoh that came into the sea after them; there remained not so much as one of them.

But the children of Israel walked upon dry land in the midst of the sea, and the waters were a wall unto them on their right hand and on their left.
Thus the LORD saved Israel that day out of the hand of the Egyptians, and Israel saw the Egyptians dead upon the sea shore.
And Israel saw that great work which the LORD did upon the Egyptians, and the people feared the LORD, and believed the LORD and his servant Moses (Exodus 14:26-31).

## Red Sea Experience

"That the trial of your faith, being much more precious than of gold that perisheth, though it be tried with fire, might be found unto praise and honour and glory at the appearing of Jesus Christ..." (I Peter 1:7).

What is a "Red Sea Experience"? By my definition, it is an experience that takes you to a place where you have no choice but to trust God or die. You will either sink or swim. You cannot go forward, backward, to the left or to the right. You just have to "stand still and see the salvation of the Lord" (Exodus 14:13). Have you ever had that type of experience?

Let's look at the life of Abraham. He was tested to the core. The test was not to trip him up and watch him fall but to deepen his capacity to obey and thus to develop his character. Just as fire refines ore to extract precious metals, God refines us through difficult circumstances. Genesis 22:1-2 says:

And it came to pass after these things, that God

> did tempt (test) Abraham, and said unto him, Abraham, and he said, Behold, here I am.
> And he said, Take now thy son, thine only son Isaac, whom thou lovest, and get thee into the land of Moriah and offer him there for a burnt offering upon one of the mountains which I will tell thee of.

This was not Abraham's first test of faith. God instructed Abraham to leave his family and home in Haran to go to an unnamed place (Genesis 12). Faith was also demonstrated when he was content in the land of Canaan while Lot lived among the cities of the plain (Genesis 13). Faith was present when he pursued and defeated the kings who took Lot captive and refused the homage of the king of Sodom (Genesis 14).

However, Abraham's faith was not always constant. For instance, fear got the better of him before Pharaoh (Genesis 12:11-20) and Abimelech (Genesis 20:2-13) when he told them Sarah was his sister – allowing both of these kings to threaten the very union out of which the promised child was to be born. And, Abraham failed to trust in God and His promises when he took Hagar as a concubine (Genesis 16:1-4). But the request to obey and trust God required great faith:

> And Abraham rose up early in the morning, and saddled his ass, and took two of his young men with him, and Isaac his son, and clave the wood for the burnt offering, and rose up, and went unto the place of which God had told him.
> Then on the third day Abraham lifted up his eyes, and saw the place afar off.
> And Abraham said unto his young men, Abide ye here with the ass, and I and the lad will go yonder and worship and come again to you (Genesis 22:3-5).

Abraham performed one of the greatest acts of obedience in recorded history. He had to learn many tough lessons about the importance of obeying God. This time his obedience was prompt and complete.

Obeying God is often a struggle because it may mean giving up something we truly want. We should not expect our obedience to God to always be easy or to come naturally at first. Hebrews 5:8 says, "Though He were a Son, yet learned He obedience by the things which He suffered." Christ's struggle in His flesh to "let this cup pass from Me…" ultimately had to end with, "nevertheless not as I will, but as thou wilt" (Matthew 26:39). And because of His obedience "… shall many be made righteous" (Romans 5:19).

Abraham **fully expected** to come back with Isaac: "**I and the lad will go yonder and worship and come again to you**" (Genesis 22:5). He expected to come back with Isaac even though he had a clear command from God to sacrifice him as a burnt offering. Hebrews 11:17-19 offers an inspired comment on Abraham's faith:

> By faith Abraham, when he was tried, offered up Isaac: and he that had received the promises offered up his only begotten son,
> Of whom it was said, That in Isaac shall thy seed be called:
> Accounting that God was able to raise him up, even from the dead from whence also he received him in a figure.

Abraham had faith, not just in God's power but also in His promise to raise the dead. Even if Isaac died at his hands, he believed that God could bring him back to life. His faith was supported by his actions:

> Was not Abraham our father justified by works, when he had offered Isaac his son upon the altar? Seest thou how faith wrought with his works, and by works was faith made perfect? (James 2:21-22).

Genesis continues:

> And Abraham took the wood of the burnt offering, and laid it upon Isaac his son, and he took the fire in his hand, and a knife, and they went both of them together.
> And Isaac spake unto Abraham his father, and said, My father, and he said, Here am I, my son. And he said, Behold the fire and the wood, but where is the lamb for a burnt offering?
> And Abraham said, My son, God will provide himself a lamb for a burnt offering, so they went both of them together (Genesis 22:6-8).

In Leviticus 20, God condemned the sacrifice of children, but we see here that He has asked Abraham to sacrifice His son. God did not want Isaac to die, but he wanted Abraham to sacrifice Isaac in his heart so it would be clear that he loved God more than he loved the promise. He could not "worship and serve the creature more than the Creator" (Romans 1:25). This was a difficult experience, but Abraham strengthened his commitment to obey God. He also learned a valuable lesson that God would provide:

> And they came to the place which God had told him of, and Abraham built an altar there, and laid the wood in order, and bound Isaac his son, and laid him on the altar upon the wood.
> And Abraham stretched forth his hand and took the knife to slay his son.

And the angel of the LORD called unto him out of heaven, and said, Abraham, Abraham, and he said, Here am I.

And he said, Lay not thine hand upon the lad, neither do thou any thing unto him. For now I know that thou fearest God, seeing thou hast not withheld thy son, thine only son from me.

And Abraham lifted up his eyes, and looked, and behold behind him a ram caught in a thicket by his horns: and Abraham went and took the ram, and offered him up for a burnt offering in the stead of his son.

And Abraham called the name of that place Jehovah-jireh: as it is said to this day, In the mount of the LORD it shall be seen (Genesis 22:9-14).

Can you see the parallel between the ram being offered instead of Isaac and Christ being offered for sin instead of us? God prevented Abraham from sacrificing his son but did not spare His own Son, Jesus, from dying on the cross. He sent His only begotten Son to die for us so that we would be spared from the eternal death that we deserve.

# 9

## My Red Sea Experience

On January 15, 2005 my faith was tested with my oldest son. We received a call that morning around 1:30 a.m. The person on the other line asked if we had talked to André. We had no idea what was going on. My husband answered the phone, and they told him that someone had attacked André and beaten him up. Another call came shortly after that, and we were told that he had been taken to the hospital. Then my grandmother called and said that the police had been to her house and that André was at the hospital because someone had beaten him up pretty badly. After we got off the phone with her, someone else called and said that his brain was hanging out of his head and that he might not make it. Well, immediately, I jumped out of bed and got dressed to go to the hospital. I awakened my youngest son, Brint, to drive me to the hospital about 22 miles away in Concord. My husband stayed behind to answer the calls that were coming in. We were pretty upset and started praying. While on the way to the hospital, I explained to Brint what was told to us over the phone and that I really was not sure what happened. I do know that before we left, André's wife had called, and she was on her way to the hospital also.

We reached the hospital within 30 minutes and entered

through the emergency room. The staff took us to a room where other family members and some close friends had gathered. There was also a police officer there, and I thanked him for taking care of the matter. He said to me that it did not make sense for anyone to have been beaten as André was. I told the officer that I knew my son had given them some problems in the past, but I appreciated their help. We sat in this room waiting to hear from the doctors. Other staff members were heard saying, "**If he makes it through the night it would be a miracle.**" They told us there was a 50-50 chance for André. They did not know that we knew a Doctor who could help him make it through the night. The family and friends prayed. Yet there were some that were very angry and crying. We knew that it was not like André to hurt anybody. He would give you the shirt off his back if you needed it. In our minds, we wanted to know what type of person would do this. How could you continuously hit someone in the head with a brick unless you were trying to kill him? It was evident that this was the culprit's intention.

We heard all kinds of stories. The first was that this person was hiding in a friend's closet. The culprit came out of the closet and hit him with a brick and then stomped on his head. Then someone said my son was invited to another person's home, and when he arrived, the culprit went in behind him, hit him in the head with something, and Andre fell to the floor. Then the young man just kept kicking him in the head. Then the young man went outside, and bystanders held him back to prevent him from going back inside. Some even heard him ask, "Is he dead yet?" A lot of people said this was a set-up. The third story was that this young man just came up and hit André unexpectedly. There were so many stories that I did not know what to believe. I cannot tell you the number of stories that were told of how the incident happened. I do know this, God knows what really happened, and whatever is done in the dark will truly come to the light. We were told by some that they were going to leave my son in the place where he was attacked and lock the door.

## Dr. Linda Smith

He would have died if someone had not intervened. Some neighbors next door heard the commotion in the house and knocked on the door. His attacker was not going to let them in but the neighbors saw someone lying on the floor, pushed their way in, saw who it was, and called the police.

It was now approaching 6:30 a.m. at the hospital, and we still hadn't seen André. They had transferred him to the Intensive Care Unit, and we had to wait another hour before we could see him. When we were allowed to go in, André s mother-in-law and I went in first. It was awful to see him lying there with all those tubes and monitors. The surgeon had to bore a hole in his skull to monitor the swelling in his brain, and he was breathing with the help of a ventilator. The diagnosis was severe: closed head injury, contusions, subdural hematoma, pneumonia, tracheostomy dependent, hyponatremia, leukocytosis, and keratopathy.

After all the family members that were present had seen him the tears flowed, and anger was aroused. However, the saints of God had to get their composure. God gave me the strength at that time to comfort the others. Later on, I wanted to scream and cry, but I just could not. My faith kicked in. Naturally, I wanted to hurt someone, but I knew in my heart, my Father, God, would fight my battle for me. I belong to the royal priesthood, and I am about doing my Father's business. How many of you know that when you do what God wants you to do, He will take care of you?

I thought about the times I had been there for my son. We had prayed for him, and he was raised in the church but he was not serving the Lord. In Proverbs 22:6, it says to, "Train up a child in the way he should go; and when he is old he will not depart from it." I prayed for him, his dad prayed for him, and we wanted him to be saved and serve the Lord. As a mother, evangelist, and a pastor's wife, I wanted our children to be good children in the

Lord. All good parents want the best for their children. We have to realize that we may want them to be like us and serve the Lord, but, ultimately, it is up to them. We can suggest that they serve the Lord and can desire it to the utmost, but if it is not in their hearts, they will not serve the Lord until they are ready. I'm not saying that you should stop praying for them, but this is a walk that they have to take. We cannot walk it for them.

A wise note to you as people of God: you have to be careful what you ask God for. I knew my son had a calling on his life from when he was a child. But he did not want to surrender to God. We told André that it was imperative that he serve the Lord. I told the Lord, "However you bring him in, Lord it is all right with me!" I asked Him not to kill him but to bring him in, no matter what it took. You may say, why did you say that? There are a lot of reasons why I said this. When you're a parent, you want your child to do what's right. It was in my heart for him to do right, but not in his. When it is not in your children's heart, they will only get saved or act saved while around you. We, as parents, have to realize that if they get saved for us, it will not last. However, when they truly give their heart to Christ, you will know that it is real.

My son had been in trouble with the law. He was the type of child who would get in trouble to help someone else. He was a loving person. As long as people surrounded him, he was a happy camper. He would never hurt anyone. He would take his last of anything to help someone. He would allow himself to suffer to help someone else in need.

When he was a child he went to the store for me and gave my change to someone else in lieu of bringing it back. We asked for the change, and he lied, so we had to punish him. Later we found out that someone else needed the money and he gave it to them. We told him if he had told us the truth it would have prevented him from being punished and getting a whipping. We love our children with all our hearts, but we must teach them to tell the truth no matter what the consequences are.

In all that we do we must realize that God is the head (the real daddy) and that He just lent us these children. I woke up to the fact that God is the head and that He allowed me to have these children for a while.

Let's get back to the hospital. After we had seen André, we left the hospital at 8:30 a.m. to go home to try to get some rest. However, it was hard to sleep because my mind was wandering. The Youth Department of the church was having a play that night, and my youngest son, Brint, was in it. Therefore, my husband and I needed to be there. You know the enemy will play games with your mind. Let me tell you, the enemy wanted me to just sit there, cry, and worry over the situation. Yes, I could sit there and let my mind wonder, "where did I go wrong?" or "What could I have done to prevent this from happening?" Sitting around thinking about what has happened can cause the enemy to play with your mind and plant all kinds of thoughts in your head.

The next day was André's thirty-fifth birthday, and he was lying in the hospital not knowing he existed in this world. His birthday fell on a Sunday, so we were at church when my pastor, my husband, announced what had happen to our son. Something on the inside of me wanted to burst out in tears, but I knew the Word, and I knew God would not let me go through this if I was not able to handle it.

The latter part of I Corinthians 10:13 says, "...but God *is* faithful, who will not suffer you to be tempted above that ye are able; but will with the temptation also make a way to escape, that ye may be able to bear *it*." I knew that while we were at church doing God's work, God was taking care of our son.

I went to the hospital on that following Monday and sat with my family and friends. All we could do was sit around and talk with each other. There was nothing we could do. People were calling the hospital trying to find out if he was dead or alive. Some of his associates came by the hospital to see how he was doing and wanted to go back to the room to see him. But due to the episode on Sunday, we could not let everyone see him because the pressure in his head was increasing. You see, the doctor thought because people were constantly going in the room and talking to him might have caused the pressure in his brain to increase along with his blood pressure. They thought he could hear and was not able to say anything, and this could cause more harm. While sitting in the waiting room, all types of people came to see him. I really thanked God for all of the Pastors and all of the people of God, People of Prayer and Faith, who came to pray for André. You can never have enough prayer. At this point in time I still told God, "Let your will be done."

On January 19th, I went to school as usual. When I got to school, some had heard that he was dead. You know people will say different things and really don't know the facts. Then I went to the hospital to see how my son was doing. He was still lying there not knowing that he was in the world.

On this day I started letting my faith waiver because of the lifestyle of my son. One minute he was in the church, and the next he was out doing his own thing. I still told God, "Let your will be done." That meant if He had to take him, it was OK with me, but that I would like to speak to Andre because I wanted to make sure he knew the Lord before he died. You may say how do you know that he did not confess while lying there? I did not know, but I do know that God does not hear a sinner's prayer unless it is for repentance. John 9:31 says, "Now we know that God heareth not sinners..." I really did not want my son to die and go to hell. During this time the devil played a game with me for a short period. The enemy had me thinking I was giving my son to God for selfish reasons, and I began to think that. I asked God how I could do His work and have to constantly wonder what was going to happen next? I made a vow to the Lord that I would do His work no matter what happened. That meant if He took my child then I could and would accept it. I wanted so much for my son to live for the Lord. André had to want this also. I was standing on the Word that my seed would be saved. All this was going on in my mind while he was lying there filled with those tubes, not knowing if he was going to make it. The saints of God were praying. There is power in prayer. I know that prayer can change things. Look at Hezekiah. He prayed, and God prolonged his life fifteen years (2 Kings 20:1-11). I know for myself what prayer can do.

Over the next couple of weeks, I would go to the hospital and see our son lying there with no response. We knew God was there all the time, and we knew our time was not God's time. However, we were still human, and we wanted to see some quick results. As time went on, my son's wife told me that he moved his hand and tried to open his eyes. I could never get him to respond to me, and then one day he did. The day that he responded to me I was happy, yet sad. Sometime after that he began moving his body more. It was sort of scary because we did not know if he was in pain. We really could not tell what was going on due to the injuries and all the medicine he was on. To tell you the truth, I was a little scared because I was not sure how delicate he was. They had put some restraints on him so that he would not pull the tubes out. They had to put a tracheotomy tube in his throat to help him breath because the ventilator had caused pneumonia to settle in one of his lungs. They tried to prevent it from settling in the other lung but, unfortunately, it was unavoidable. Once the tracheotomy tube was in we knew he would not be able to talk. They also had to put a feeding tube in him.

The day came when he was taken out of intensive care and put him in a room. The prayers of the righteous avail much: "...The effectual fervent prayer of a righteous man or woman availeth much" (James 5:16). God had blessed him and us! They were giving him some rehabilitation even though they knew that he would have to be transferred somewhere else. Always remember, God is still in control no matter what it looks like. We gave God praise for what He had already done. You see, we must give Him praise even when we are going through trials and tribulations. See what the Lord had done! Here was my son lying in a bed, not completely understanding what we are saying to him, and he could only make a few sounds and gestures. I thank God for the sounds because at one point they did not think he was going to make it. Just look at God! If God can speak to some dead bones, and they come alive, then why cannot I believe God to bring our son back to normal? If Ezekiel can speak to those dry bones, then why cannot I believe God for my son?

> The hand of the LORD was upon me, and carried me out in the spirit of the LORD, and set me down in the midst of the valley which was full of bones,
> And caused me to pass by them round about: and, behold, there were very many in the open valley; and, lo, they were very dry.
> And he said unto me, Son of man, can these bones live? And I answered, O Lord GOD, thou knowest.
> Again he said unto me, Prophesy upon these bones, and say unto them, O ye dry bones, hear the word of the LORD.
> Thus saith the Lord GOD unto these bones; Behold, I will cause breath to enter into you, and ye shall live:
> And I will lay sinews upon you, and will bring up flesh upon you, and cover you with skin, and put

breath in you, and ye shall live; and ye shall know that I am the LORD.

So I prophesied as I was commanded: and as I prophesied, there was a noise, and behold a shaking, and the bones came together, bone to his bone.

And when I beheld, lo, the sinews and the flesh came up upon them, and the skin covered them above: but there was no breath in them.

Then said he unto me, Prophesy unto the wind, prophesy, son of man, and say to the wind, Thus saith the Lord GOD; Come from the four winds, O breath, and breathe upon these slain, that they may live.

So I prophesied as he commanded me, and the breath came into them, and they lived, and stood up upon their feet, an exceeding great army.

Then he said unto me, Son of man, these bones are the whole house of Israel: behold, they say, Our bones are dried, and our hope is lost: we are cut off for our parts.

Therefore prophesy and say unto them, Thus saith the Lord GOD; Behold, O my people, I will open your graves, and cause you to come up out of your graves, and bring you into the land of Israel.

And ye shall know that I am the LORD, when I have opened your graves, O my people, and brought you up out of your graves,

And shall put my spirit in you, and ye shall live, and I shall place you in your own land: then shall ye know that I the LORD have spoken it, and performed it, saith the LORD (Ezekiel 37:1-14).

God can do anything but fail. This was something simple for God. I say simple because nothing is too hard for the God I serve. You know in baseball, you have minor and major leagues. I consider this as the bridge between the minor and the major. At our church we have been saying, "Lord, don't let my faith fail me in the time of testing." This was a test that I wanted to pass. I John 4:4 says, "…because greater is He that is in you, than he that is in the world." Because God lives inside of me, I'm "more than a conqueror" (Romans 8:37). I know God as a healer, and I knew that our son would fully recover and be back to normal.

On February 4, 2005, our son went to a rehabilitation facility. They had to order a tent bed for him. The tent was to prevent him from hitting his head or falling out of the bed. With this bed you had to zip him in and out. They would sit him in a wheelchair and take him to therapy and try to get him to stand up and hold his head up. André could not sit up without being strapped in. Neither could he stand on his own. They had to help him at all times. While visiting, I noticed that while in the wheel chair he was putting his hand up to his mouth as if he was drinking something. At first I did not understand what he was doing, but he kept on doing this for a couple of days, and finally it dawned on me that he wanted a drink of water. We told him that he could not have water with the tracheotomy tube in his throat, not knowing if he really understood that or not.

With the band wrapped around him, André had started sitting up in the wheelchair. Even though he could not sit up on his own, he was moving his body, leaning forward and wrestling to get out of the chair. You know it is hard to see your child like that. The day finally came when he started moving around with some activity and knew what was going on! You could see how the Lord was moving on his behalf. André had begun putting forth an effort with the rehabilitation nurses whereas before he was not even trying to get up on his own. His rehab nurse was really pleased with him. Naturally, they thought it was because of what they were doing, but we knew it was because of God. André kept on holding his hand up like he was drinking water, but he could not have water. He wanted the tracheotomy tube to come out because he wanted something to drink and eat. We had to tell him he must pass his swallowing test before he can get anything to eat or drink. He took his test on a Wednesday and passed it! They put him on mechanical soft foods in lieu of pureed foods. Most people, when taking the tracheotomy tube out, go straight to pureed foods. That evening he was brought some soft foods, and he was eating and drinking like he had never had anything in his throat! In fact, he was eating so much because he could not get full! It appeared to me he was trying to make up for lost time. This young man wanted double portions of food, and they gave it to him! The doctor advised André's wife that his appetite might be coming from the medicines that he was on and that it would go away with time. André loves coffee, and they would have to go get him coffee all the time!

The doctors and nurses were amazed at André's progress. They knew how he was when he came in and what they had been working with. It seems as if overnight God stepped in and brought life back into him. They worked more intensely with him after they saw a change because they knew he was on his way back. Although André was coming around, he would say things like, "Dale Earnhardt was in my room last night and the D.E.I. (Dale Earnhardt Insurance) is paying my bill. We have to do what D.E.I. said to do." We tried to tell him that D.E.I. had nothing to do with him, and he declared that he worked for Dale at one time and that Dale had told him that they were holding his job for him. This concerned us because we knew Dale had not been to see him nor did he ever work for him. We noticed that is what he saw on TV was what he was talking about. Once you have a brain injury that can happen. It was difficult to see my child talk "out of his head." We knew that God would take care of this also because He's not a God that does things half way.

On March 23, 2005, I was in school and got a call from my son's caseworker telling me that he needed to speak to me. In the meantime (while still in school) my phone started to vibrate. I knew it was someone else calling regarding my son. After class I went to my car and checked my voice mail. It was my husband calling me to tell me what the caseworker had to say. Well, I was on my way to the hospital. While in route to the hospital I tried to call the caseworker but was unsuccessful in reaching him. I called my husband back to see what was going on, and he indicated that it was time for our son to leave the rehabilitation hospital. The caseworker wanted to know where Andre was going to be living. I knew for a fact that André could not go back to my grandmother's. The caseworker said that he was physically able, but we had some concerns regarding his mental injuries. André was only hearing what he wanted to hear. I had already told him that we were looking for a facility to place him in. Andre flat out told me that he was going home; everyone at the hospital told him he was ready! You talk about being in a hole and cannot get out – that's how I felt because no matter what I would say, what was stuck in his brain was that they told him he was OK, and he could go home, not to a facility, but home. Here comes the enemy like a flood trying to stop the flow of everything that's good. He tried to inflict pain and hurt into me. (Believe me, I was hurting because as a mom you want to do everything humanly possible for your children, even at thirty-five years of age.) After reaching the hospital I tried to call the caseworker and still could not reach him. On my way to my son's room, I reminded myself that God would not have allowed this to happen if I could not handle it. I Corinthians 10:13 says:

> There hath no temptation taken you but such as is common to man: but God is faithful, who will not suffer you to be tempted above that you are able; but will with the temptation also make a way to escape, that ye may be able to bear it.

When I reached my son's room I saw that he was in good spirits. This was because he told me he was going home and that it was approved. They, the staff, had talked with my Aunt and Grandmother. This caught me off guard because I did not know the hospital was going to call them. My grandmother just had her ninety-fourth birthday in May. She was not in the best of health but had a sharp mind. My Aunt was taking care of my grandmother and was not well either, and she could not handle the responsibility of my son. I would never think of asking them to take on that responsibility, and, quite frankly, I was upset that the caseworker called them without touching base with Andre's wife or me. You see, most of the time my son did well, but with the type of brain injury that he had sustained, he could relapse at any time, and they would not have any control. What thirty-five-year-old man wants two old ladies telling him that he cannot do something when in his mind he feels he can do what he wants? I could see that my son needed help, and he did not believe he did. While André was in speech therapy that day, I went to look for the caseworker. Only God could help me at this time because I felt like a hopeless chicken about to have its neck wrung and could not do anything to prevent it. I had to face the reality that I could not send André back where he was before the incident and that it would be a good thing for him to go to a facility. The caseworker asked me why could not I take him in? I told him that we were in ministry and not at home all the time to watch him. The enemy wanted me to feel guilt about putting him in a nursing home. Oh yes, I did feel guilty, but I knew I had done all I could do and that I had to do God's work, also. God's work was and is very important to me, and I want to do all I can for the Lord. This does not mean that I have forsaken my family, but I have repeatedly sacrificed for my children and family for a long time. I know my joy comes from the Lord, and I want to keep that joy in what I am doing for him. Sometimes we carry the weights of others when we don't have to.

Today, André is in his second marriage, has just purchased a home and is doing quite well. The doctors were amazed at the progress that he made. My faith comes from hearing the word of God and letting it soak into my heart/spirit. It is like a dry dishrag that has been put in water to soak up the water; I want all God has for me. I know my God is working on my behalf for André. When the doctor's said he would not make it, the prayers of the righteous went up, and God heard those prayers. Look at what the Lord has done for my son.

If we began to tell all that God has done we would never get to the end. God is good and greatly to be praised! I give Him all the honor and glory for what He has done for our son. This was a Red Sea Experience for me. I had to believe against hope that my son would be OK. Though the water seemed deep, and crossing it seemed an impossibility, I had to believe that God would give us a miracle and allow us to cross over. As André continued to improve, it let me know that we were crossing on dry ground, even though I could see the walls of water all around us. We made it through. Like I said, the doctors were amazed at his progress. After his last appointment, the doctor talked about how sharp he was. Someone even said, "If I did not know, I would never have thought that he was so badly beaten. God is just awesome! He took my son from a hopeless state to where he is right now, and I am truly grateful.

# 10

## With Faith I Can Make It

"I can do all things through Christ which strengheneth me" (Philippians 4:13). There are times in our life when we feel as if we cannot make it and even feel like giving up. Maybe you have never felt this way. There have been times when I had to face obstacles, and I wanted to run and hide. I really did not want to deal with the situation at that particular time. Sometimes I felt like I was the toilet and that it was time to be flushed. I was too full to handle the circumstances that surrounded me. When the cares of life weigh you down you have to have crazy faith to know that God can and will deliver you. Psalm 46:1 says, "God is our refuge and strength, a very present help in trouble."

### When the Storm Comes in Like a Flood

Have you ever watched it rain? Let your mind wonder and see the drizzling rain. Then, all of a sudden, it appears as though the floodgates have been opened because the rain is pouring down. The enemy comes in like a flood sometimes. The enemy will put every obstacle he can in your way to stop you. We might say that we must be doing something right because the enemy (the devil) would not attack us the way he has. Let me explain something. If we were not trying to live right, the enemy would have no reason to mess with us because he would already have us. Why would a dog want a steak bone when he could have the steak? If we are doing all that we can for the Lord, then we are a nuisance to the devil. He wants to stop us any way he can. That's why it is important to put on the full armor of God. In fact, we should sleep with our armor on so that the enemy cannot attack us while we are sleeping. Ephesians 6:10-17 says:

> Finally, my brethren, be strong in the Lord, and in the power of his might.
> Put on the whole armour of God, that ye may be able to stand against the wiles of the devil.
> For we wrestle not against flesh and blood, but against principalities, against powers, against the rulers of the darkness of this world, against spiritual wickedness in high places.
> Wherefore take unto you the whole armour of God, that ye may be able to withstand in the evil day, and having done all, to stand.
> Stand therefore, having your loins girt about with truth, and having on the breastplate of righteousness;
> And your feet shod with the preparation of the gospel of peace;
> Above all, taking the shield of faith, wherewith ye shall be able to quench all the fiery darts of the wicked.
> And take the helmet of salvation, and the sword of the Spirit, which is the word of God...

# Dr. Linda Smith

## He Will Not Let Go

The enemy has been on my trail for some time now, trying to weigh me down. The scripture tells me to lay down every weight:

> Wherefore seeing we also are compassed about with so great a cloud of witnesses, let us lay aside every weight, and the sin which doth so easily beset us, and let us run with patience the race that is set before us... (Hebrews 12:1)

The enemy wants me to throw in the towel, but I will not because 1 John 4:4 says, "...because greater is He that is in you, than he that is in the world." Because Jesus lives on the inside of me I do not fear what the enemy tries to do.

When I was trying to get my Doctorate in Theology, I had to take classes plus read extra reference material. I had to have some crazy faith to believe I could accomplish this in such a time constraint. I would like for you to understand that I am married, a mother and an Evangelist, therefore, my days are pretty complete. I do not have any small children, but my family does rely on me. Not only my family but also, I'm the pastor's wife, the First Lady. I do not sit around looking cute. At the time, I taught bible classes for the women at our church. We had classes every second, third, and fourth Tuesday nights of the month. In order to teach class, I had to prepare for class, so as you can see, my plate was pretty full.

My "Red Sea Experience" with Andre took place while I was taking classes for my doctorate and teaching Bible classes at the church. After Andre left the hospital he went to a nursing home in Albemarle, NC, which was a good distance from where I lived. I visited him two or three times a week. My schedule was full, but I thank God for grace and mercy. My entire schedule was as follows:

1. Sundays - in church all day because we have morning and evening services.

2. Tuesdays at the Kannapolis Church all day and some nights because of the classes and sometimes because of counseling sessions with members.

3. Wednesdays - I would have a Theology class in the morning and Bible study in the evening at the Rock Hill Church.

4. Thursdays - I would get my hair done or go and spend a couple hours with André.

5. Fridays – They were supposed to be a day for me and my husband. Most of the time we did get to go out to dinner, but there were times that we could not spend time together due to circumstances.

6. Saturdays – We have corporate prayer the first Saturday of every month. Sometimes there were revivals or conferences planned or we would have appointments to preach at other churches. There would be times when we would be on the road for four days straight.

When you are on the road it is very hard to get done what you need to such as reading for class. I would take my books with me and might only get to read five to ten pages, if that much. As you can see I'm not a lady of leisure. While trying to obtain my doctorate, I still continued my full-time duties as an Evangelist, preaching the Word of God on some Sundays, hosting Women's Conferences and other speaking engagements. God always gave me the strength to do what He wanted me to do. I was not lying around complaining about what I was going through. I learned a long time ago that there is someone somewhere in worse shape than I am. Don't get me wrong. There were times when I just wanted to throw in the towel, get a hotel room, and not tell anyone where I was and spend some quality time by myself. There were times I wished no one knew my name. I felt like I was between a rock and a hard place and could not move. I would wonder, "God where are you? Don't you know this is your child who needs help?" But timing is everything with God. Psalm 34:19 says, "Many are the afflictions of the righteous: but the Lord delivereth him out of them all."

God is so good, and we cannot thank Him enough for what He has done. I can truly say, "If it had not been for the Lord on my side where would I be?" A songwriter wrote, "I've been through the storm, and I've been through the rain, but I made it."

## Here He Comes Again

While in the midst of everything, my grandmother became ill. As soon as they get her back to par they called my Aunt, who takes care of her, to let her know that while she was in the hospital they felt a lump in her breast. My grandmother was ninety-three when they first diagnosed her with breast cancer. Because of her frail state, she was not able to handle chemotherapy or radiation. They wanted to run more tests on her, but she said no. My grandmother was a believer and said she was ready for the Lord. She believed in miracles and healings because she has had miracles before. God had been good to her and had healed her body on several occasions. Isaiah 53:5 says:

But he was wounded for our transgressions, he was bruised for our iniquities: the chastisement of our peace was upon him; and with his stripes we are healed.

I Peter 2: 24 says,

Who his own self bare our sins in his own body on the tree, that we, being dead to sins, should live unto righteousness: by whose stripes ye were healed.

If she had to die with cancer, I know God is still a healer. We have to remember <u>God will not go over our will</u>.

## He is Going for the Knock Out

Apparently, this book is going to encourage someone. I started writing this as my dissertation for graduation. I had to have crazy faith to know that God and I will get this paper done on time with all the barriers that had been in my way. I want to give God all the praise and honor because, through it all, He has kept me.

In the latter part of May 2005, my mother-in-law who we called Ma Ma and who I loved as much as my mom, fell and broke her kneecap. This was the same knee that she had had replaced some years before. She had to have surgery and came through it with flying colors. She did her rehabilitation in a nursing home. This was a great woman of faith, one who I did not mind following anywhere she went because she was a woman of integrity, and she loved the Lord with all her heart. I thanked God for her.

# Dr. Linda Smith

As I said before, our son, André, had been attacked and had severe brain trauma. On June 1, 2005, while working on my dissertation, the day started out hectic. I was writing, and the phone was constantly ringing. It seemed as though someone said, "Let's call the pastor's house today." I'm normally not at home on Wednesdays because of class. The phone seemed to ring all day.

We were in the process of opening another church in Monroe, NC, and we had to meet with the owner at 1:00 p.m. If you are like me, once I start something I would like to have the opportunity to complete it. Unfortunately, the phone or my husband was a constant interruption. I tried to continue writing, but I had an important errand that I needed to do before going to Monroe. I stopped writing and did what I had to do. The meeting in Monroe went well. On the way back, I decided to stop to get something for dinner since I was able to stay home, not attend Bible Study in Rock Hill, and work on my paper. My husband talked with the secretary at the church and she told him that I really needed to stay home and work on my paper, and so I did. Thank God for an understanding husband, one who loves me.

It was about 9:00 p.m. when the phone rang again, but this time it was André. He did not seem like himself, so I asked him what was wrong. He indicated that a CNA (Certified Nurse Assistant) at the nursing home came to him out of the blue and asked him if he knew Tony. We will call him Tony so as not to reveal his true identity. I don't know if he told the CNA whether he did or not, but this disturbed my son because Tony was the guy who assaulted him. This caused his head to hurt, and the nurse went to get him something. When she returned, I was still talking with him and asked to speak to her. I told her why his head was hurting. The CNA had told André that he had been in jail with Tony. This was disturbing news to me, and it was trying to block my path from writing. The devil was and is a liar. The nurse assured me that they would take care of my son, however, earlier that day I had received a call from the District Attorney's office stating that Tony had pleaded guilty to the assault, and the official told me how long Tony had to stay in prison for felony assault. It just seemed strange to get a call from the District Attorney's office about Tony and then find out that night that someone is asking André about Tony, too. The nursing home can only watch him for a while, but I have a doctor, a nurse, and a guard who will protect him at all times if he will believe. I knew that it was done in Jesus name. Psalm 23 says,

> The LORD is my shepherd; I shall not want.
> He maketh me lie down in green pastures: He leadeth me beside the still waters.
> He restoreth my soul: He leadeth me in the paths of righteousness for his name's sake.
> Yea, though I walk through the valley of the shadow of death, I will fear no evil: for thou art with me; thy rod and thy staff they comfort me.
> Thou preparest a table before me in the presence of mine enemies: thou anointest my head with oil; my cup runneth over.
> Surely goodness and mercy shall follow me all the days of my life: and I will dwell in the house of the LORD for ever.

# 11

## A Friend In Distress

There is a lady who I know that had her world turned upside down. If it were not for her faith and trust in God, she believes she never would have made it. She and her husband were believers but were having difficulty communicating with one another. They sought counseling but when the husband did not like what the counselor said to him, he decided not to go back. Of course, the problems continued and discussions would turn into arguments, and the arguments usually led to one of the parties leaving the room. Leaving the room soon turned into her husband not coming home after work. He would come in late or not at all.

All the while this was going on, she was praying. She had gotten weary of her treatment at home because when they got to church, everyone was always complimenting him or telling her how wonderful he was. She would always smile and thank them for the compliment, but deep inside she was hurting and did not know what to do. There were no close friends that she could talk to. They were always moving around on the East coast because of his job, so there were no lasting friendships. The pastor of the church they attended only preached about drugs and alcohol, so she really felt no connection with him either.

## Crazy Faith

Her husband, we will call him Johnny so as not to reveal his true identity, loved to invite other believers to their home for dinner on Sunday afternoons. He worked Monday – Friday and would hang out with "his boys" on Saturdays. He had an office job, 7:00 a.m. until 4:00 p.m, and would come home and talk about the "good" time he had at work. (We will call her Mary so as not to reveal her true identity.) Mary did not mind the company on Sundays as long as she knew ahead of time that they were coming. Mary worked in a machine shop, and every four weeks she rotated from working first shift to third shift. This was strenuous work because she had to stand on a hard cement floor for eight hours and run a machine that manufactured brakes for trains. If something went wrong with the machine, she was responsible for fixing it. By the time her shift was over she would be greasy and dirty and would have metal chips in her hair and clothing.

Because Mary knew that her husband enjoyed the fellowship of other believers on Sunday afternoons, she would go out of her way to make sure she prepared enough food for everyone, prepare things that she knew they would enjoy, and made sure the afternoon was an enjoyable one for all. Mary would ask her husband to let her know whenever he wanted to have guests because previously he would give no advance warning. People would just show-up. He agreed to let her know ahead of time, and this worked out pretty well. But then, things went back to the "norm," and he would ask friends over for dinner without telling her. Mary explained that she was really having a hard time trying to keep up with his whims. (I forgot to mention that they had a toddler who Mary took care of with very little help from Johnny.)

One Sunday, after teaching Children's Church, Mary headed for the car to go home. The kids had seemed to wear her out, and problems at home seemed to weigh her down. She also had to go to work that night and needed to rest. Her schedule had rotated, and she knew she had to be at work by 11:00 p.m. that night. The house needed to be cleaned, dinner needed to be prepared, and she had to take a nap in order to be able to stay awake all night. All of these things were going through her mind as she was strapping their toddler in the car seat. Johnny approached the car and explained that he had just invited a family over for dinner. Well, something must have snapped because Mary turned to him and said, "If you want to have guests over today, then go home, clean up, prepare the meal, entertain your guests, watch the baby, and clean up after everyone because I'm going to bed! I have to work tonight!" That must have gotten his attention! They rode home in separate cars. After they both got home, no one showed up. He told her later because she was so "nasty" he told his guests not to come. At that point she did not care what anyone thought.

I need to interject here that these two people are believers. Neither one of them, up to this point, had said to one another, "We need to bring our marriage to God in prayer!" All of the petty things that were happening allowed the enemy to have access into their lives. If anyone was praying, it was not evident. If anyone had been reading the Word, it was not evident. But Mary said during this time she was praying but not reading the Word like she should have. She also said that all of the pettiness could have been prevented if both of them had been in the spiritual place where God wanted them. She felt she was always walked over, and he felt because he was the head of the house whatever he said was the final word with no discussion. Johnny even said that he tried to talk to one of the brethren who was a minister, but that turned out to be a disaster! After he talked to that minister, everyone in church knew that they were having problems. Even a deacon approached Johnny and said something derogatory towards him. Because Johnny would have friendly conversations with various members after church, he was accused of flirting with other women when they found out they were having problems.

Where is the body of Christ when you need it? They say don't go to the world for help or advice. If this church represented the entire body of Christ, I would not go to them either!

Needless to say, things got worse for Johnny and Mary until one day Johnny backslid. He fell out of fellowship with God, began to stay out all night, and began drinking. One day he came home and told Mary that he did not want to be married to her anymore. They separated, of course, and Mary did not know what she was going to do. She was a full-time student and unemployed at the time. Their child had just turned four years old and was about to attend pre-school. All of this turmoil caused Mary to remember **Who her Strength** was.

Right before they separated she looked back on the things that had transpired and saw in the big picture of things her faith was not where it once was. She was the type of person who could believe God could do anything. If God said it, that settled it for her. It did not matter if anyone else believed it. God's Word was enough for her. Her prayer time had dwindled, and she spent very little time in the Word. When she realized where she stood with God, she repented. She had lost focus on what really mattered, and that was God. Oh yes, she knew that her family was important, but they seemed to take God's place in her life. She wanted to make her marriage work but for Johnny, it was too late. He just wanted out.

Mary continued to pray over the next year hoping her marriage would not end in divorce. During this time her confidence in God began to grow. It began to grow because she began setting time aside to read God's Word and to fast and pray for direction for her life. She still had to deal with the pain of separation though. She said sometimes she found herself crying. Then one day she decided to ask God, "When will I stop crying?" Do you know what God's response was? He said, "STOP CRYING." In other words, it was her choice. She could continue crying and feeling sorry for herself or she could stand on what He promised her in His Word. His Word says, "...I will never leave thee, not forsake thee." (Hebrews 13:5) His word says:

> Fear thou not; I am with thee: be not dismayed, for I am thy God: I will help thee; yea, I will uphold thee; With the right hand of my righteousness (Isaiah 41:10).

One would think, "Why would God be so stern with her?" I think the reason is that with our own children we know what works in order for them to see the big picture. When your children have done something that requires discipline, one child may require a spanking. Another child can commit the same offense and may only need a lecture to keep them from doing it again.

Over Mary's life, she had seen the hand of God. She knew God's Word. She was not a babe in Christ. She knew how to stand on God's Word and see the answer manifested. She could not be "babied" any longer. It was time to grow up. It was time for God to use her life for his glory. She could not be found in Hebrews 5:12:

> For when for the time ye ought to be teachers, ye have need that one teach you again which be the first principles of the oracles of God...

Well, what God said to her took effect. <u>She had to choose</u> to look up. <u>She had to choose</u> to walk in victory no matter how she felt. Galatians 5:7 says, "Ye did run well; who did hinder you that ye should not obey the truth?"

A short time later God called her to do the work of a Missionary. But during that time of growth, she was a full-time student, working and raising a child on her own. Her family helped out whenever they could, but some things she kept to herself. Some things God would not allow her to discuss. She had to learn to depend on Him. There were times when she thought that it was all just too much to bear. She was paying off a credit card that both she and her husband used, and she received no child or spousal support. A year after her separation, she began receiving child support because it was court ordered. However, she received less than what she should have gotten. Johnny said, "If you ask for more, don't even think about us getting back together." Because she was vulnerable, she was willing to accept what he chose to give her. Through it all, she had to remember that God's Word said:

> There hath no temptation taken you but such as is common to man: but God is Faithful, who will not suffer you to be tempted above that ye are able; but will with the temptation also make a way to escape, that ye may be able to bear it (I Corinthians 10:13).

God brought her through it, but she had to stand on and believe God's Word. He is able to do just what he said.

# 12

## A Sister Stepping Out On Faith

(Another Sister's Personal Journey in Her Words)

My journey to stepping out in faith started with hard times and many difficult tasks. When you start out planting a garden you have to prepare the ground by clearing rocks and tilling the soil. My ground was hard and full of rocks and drier than the desert. Now the ground was my life, and the rocks were my trials and tribulations.

Who would be willing to work with these circumstances? Many people would shake their heads and throw their hands up in the air, calling it quits.

But I did not have to do that with my God. I cried out to Him for help. I asked God to help me and to guide me. I cried out, "Lord, help me to be a servant for you."

Faith goes beyond believing. Faith is something deep down inside of me. I know that nothing can shake your faith, when you work at developing it. I had to remember what Hebrews 11:1 says, "Now faith is the substance of things hoped for, the evidence of things not seen. God's Word says, "We walk by faith not by sight." (II Corinthians 5:7). I needed that faith when my cupboards were empty, and I was not sure how I was going to get food. Psalm 37:25 says, "I have been young, and now am old; yet have I not seen the righteous forsaken, nor his seed begging bread."

The time came when I felt that nobody even cared. My children were gone, and they really had little time or nothing to do with me. Yet when they needed money they would call me. I kept asking myself, "Why? Why can't they be with me? What have I done that's so wrong? Why do I have to always be alone?" But what I was forgetting was that my God said, "…I will never leave thee, nor forsake thee" (Hebrews 13:5). God was the one who dried those tears and put joy in my heart.

My faith had to be strong while I was going through my divorce, which was supposed to be simple and uncontested but turned very nasty. If I listened to my so-called friends in the world I would have been seeking revenge. I know that God said in His Word, "Dearly beloved, avenge not yourselves, but rather give place unto wrath: for it is written, Vengeance is mine; I will repay, saith the Lord" (Romans 12:19). We leave revenge in God's hand.

> Seeing it is a righteous thing with God to recompense tribulation to them that trouble you;
> And to you who are troubled rest with us, when the Lord Jesus shall be revealed from heaven with his mighty angels (II Thessalonians 1:6-7).

People say that words cannot hurt you. Words can pierce straight through to your heart. I knew I could not make it like this, and I was going down fast. I was beginning to question why I even existed. Yet I remembered what God's Word said about me and that I am "fearfully and wonderfully made." (Psalm 139:14)

## Dr. Linda Smith

I knew God did not make junk, and I knew He had a plan for my life. I had to stay focused on Him. I could not let my faith fail me now.

No one here on earth could provide for me the way God has:

1. I was alone. He gave me a family.

2. I was lost. He provided direction.

3. I was so sad. He filled my heart with joy.

4. I was so afraid and full of fear. God gave me the peace that passes all understanding.

5. I felt so unloved. He loved me as no one else could.

6. I needed a job. He provided it.

7. I was in need of a doctor. He served as the greatest physician for me.

8. I needed a lawyer. He was my lawyer.

9. I was in need of a counselor and a teacher. He supplied them.

My faith in God has opened many doors and made provisions for me. I could look to the world, but what does it have to offer? Nothing. Having faith in God has made it easier for me to be submissive to God. These verses helped me. Faith is better than trusting man:

> I called upon the LORD in distress: the LORD answered me, *and set me* in a large place.

> The LORD *is* on my side; I will not fear: what can man do unto me?
> The LORD taketh my part with them that help me: therefore shall I see *my desire* upon them that hate me.
> It is better to trust in the LORD than to put confidence in man.
> It is better to trust in the LORD than to put confidence in princes (Psalm 118:5-9).

Faith is greater than physical strength:

> He delighteth not in the strength of the horse: he taketh not pleasure in the legs of a man.
> The LORD taketh pleasure in them that fear him, in those that hope in his mercy (Psalm 147:10-11).

My faith was tried again when I had two EKG's within a two-week time period. My blood pressure was so high they said I should not have been alive. I lay on the table while the doctors examined me, and the tears were streaming down my face. I said to myself, "I'm all alone again. What will happen if I don't make it?" I was still thinking, and I said, "Faith, I need you. The devil is a liar. I will live and not die!" God was and is my great physician. He is with me at all times. There have been so many things I've gone through such as:

1. sickness

2. divorce

3. loss of job

4. death

5. separation from my children

6. learning to like myself

7. needing a lawyer

8. financial difficulties

9. no communication with my parents

Without God I would have not made it. God loves us more than we love ourselves. You must understand, "…without faith it is impossible to please God…" (Hebrews 11:6).

You need to have faith in God. God has given each of us a measure of faith. It is up to you and me to decide to take action or not. My God doesn't force His way on anyone.

Protect your faith by keeping a close watch on what is being said around you, what you watch on television, your conversation and anything that you may be involved in. Philippians 4:8 says, "…to think on things that are pure…"

# 13

## Faith for Healing

"Before attempting to exercise faith for healing, one needs to know what the scriptures plainly teach, that it is just as much God's will to heal the body as it is to heal the soul" (Bosworth, Christ the Healer 5).

God's Word is clear on healing. James 5:14-15 says,

> Is any sick among you? let him call for the elders of the church; and let them pray over him, anointing him with oil in the name of the Lord: And the prayer of faith shall save the sick, and the Lord shall raise him up; and if he have committed sins, they shall be forgiven him.

It is God's will to heal us. Isaiah 53:5 says,

> But He was wounded for our transgressions, He was bruised for our iniquities: the chastisement of our peace was upon Him; and with His stripes we are healed.

I Peter 2:24 says,

Who His own self bare our sins in His own body on the tree that we, being dead to sins should live unto righteousness: by whose stripes you were healed.

The scripture in Isaiah says we "are healed," but Peter proclaimed ye "were healed". Christ's death was not only for our salvation but also that our bodies might be healed. How many times have you heard people say after asking God for healing, "If it be Thy will?" What have we said regarding God's will? His will is His Word. His Word says Christ died for my healing. Bosworth says, "Praying for healing with the faith destroying words, "if it be Thy will" is not planting the "seed" [God's Word]; it is destroying the seed" (Bosworth, <u>Christ the Healer</u>). We must constantly renew our minds with the Word of God for divine healing. If you meditate on God's Word and your mind is saturated with His Word, you will speak what God speaks concerning healing. Proverbs says that God's Word is life and health to our flesh. So, by constantly meditating on God's Word, we are nourishing our flesh and spirit.

## Examples of God's Word at Work

Why do we not have more miracles than healings? Miracles are instant; healings are over time. Could it be a lack of faith in the body of Christ? I believe in my heart that one day we will see the lame walk, dumb talk, deaf ears opened, blinded eyes opened, and cancers dried up. It happens in our ministry! We need to have faith like Smith Wigglesworth, Dad Mason, Katherine Kuhlman, and a great man in my day, Bishop John W. Barber.

Bishop Barber was a man of faith. I remember when I first met him. He appeared to be different from any of the other preachers that I knew. In the Bible it tells us that we should know them by their fruit. Matthew 7:20 says, "Wherefore by their fruits ye shall know them." This man of God had great faith and I would like for you to know why I say this. I saw, with my own eyes, this man pray for someone, and a miracle took place. Bishop Barber prayed for a man who was bent over due to some back problems. Bishop Barber took off his shoes. He had two men lift him up, and Bishop Barber kicked the man in the back in the name of Jesus. The man's back straightened out. Seeing this with my own eyes increased my faith because I knew if God did it for that man he could do the same for me if I ever needed it.

James 5:15-16 says:

> And the prayer of faith shall save the sick, and the Lord shall raise him up; and if he have committed sins, they shall be forgiven him.
> Confess your faults one to another, and pray one for another, that ye may be healed. The effectual fervent prayer of a righteous man availeth much.

There was a time in Bishop Barber's life that he told us about. His crew was driving him to New York, and the driver fell asleep, hit something, and the car caught on fire. Everything in the car burned except his staff and his prayer handkerchiefs. One of the men in the car was burned badly, and even though Bishop Barber was in shock, he still prayed for the burned man. To this day, you cannot tell where this young man's face had been burned.

Bishop Barber was going to New York to preach a revival, and he did not go to the hospital. He went to church and preached the Word of God. That was crazy faith! When you have been in a critical accident and you decide that you're standing on the Word of God no matter what, that's crazy faith in action!

# CRAZY FAITH

When I met Bishop Barber his body was whole, but before he left this world he had to have both of his legs amputated. This man had such great faith that he preached God's Word from his wheelchair and would say, "I can't stomp the devil out, but I can "nub" him out." I never saw or heard Bishop Barber complain about his condition. He always had a smile and was always ready to preach God's word.

I have never known anyone who has been on dialysis for most of the day and come home and preach the word that night. I talk about crazy faith, and I truly believe that Bishop Barber had that type of faith because the ordinary man would have said, "I cannot make it. I'm too weak," and would have stayed home and gotten some rest. I cannot begin to tell you of all the miracles that God did through this great man of God. Bishop Barber never stole God's glory. Someone else would say, "look at me, I healed them", when they, in themselves, could not heal a fly.

# 14

## Faith Can Travel Around the World

There is a young lady in our congregation for whom God performed the miraculous. To see her today, one would think that she was never in a terrible accident. Stationed in Germany, she became a member of one of the churches near her base. She was not saved but served as a faithful member of the church. One day the brakes on her car stopped working. The accident was horrible. Her car was a mangled mess of metal, and she lay dying. She was rushed to the emergency room. A plate had to be put in her head. Her family lived near our church, and we were asked to pray. The church in Germany was praying, too. The two churches stood on what God's Word said concerning healing, and we called those things that be not as though they were. Well, that young lady is home today. She's not crippled or handicapped. She has more energy than you can imagine. She has given her life totally to God because she realizes if it had not been for the prayers of the righteous, she would not be here today. I can truly say that her faithfulness far exceeds some members of our church who have been members for years. Every opportunity she gets, she tries to evangelize for Jesus Christ. It doesn't matter where she is, in the grocery store, in the mall, or at a local fast food restaurant. She loves sharing the Gospel with those that she meets.

And should it not be that way? We owe God so much for the things that He has done. If He never does anything else for us, we should be eternally grateful for giving His life and redeeming our souls as well as our bodies.

## Stop Fronting Faith

If there's one thing that I've learned in this walk with God is that we, as people of God, need to be real. We need to stop playing games. God already knows us. Let's take the mask off. I'm really talking to church folk because we can put on some pretty masks, ugly masks, and some strange looking masks to get our point across.

We say we have faith in God, but the minute things go wrong we get in the wrong attitude and fall apart. How many of you have ever worked a puzzle before? You know when you open the box the pieces are not put together correctly. That's how life is today. Just because I gave my life to Christ does not mean that everything fits or is perfect.

When I first got saved I thought everything was supposed to be all right, but soon after that I had a wakeup call. The Lord knew that I loved Him, and He also knew that I was looking at the people who I thought were totally committed to Him. Some of them were just "frontin'." What do I mean by "frontin?" I mean that they were pretenders. They could act, sing, and praise God while in church, but outside of church, they lived just like the sinners of the world. They did those things that an unsaved person would do. I told you how God dealt with me by telling me to take my eyes off man. I did not realize that I had started depending on these people and looking at what they were doing. Sometimes as young Christians we are not focused as we should be. Then you have "the saints" who think they know it all. They tell you what to do and when to do it. Can I help you here? We need to stay in our place until the Lord or the Pastor of the church tells us otherwise. We try to pretend to be something that we are not. Guess what, saints? Our children see how we act in the church and how we act at home. Some of us like to pretend that we have it all together and know all along that it is just a front. We try to fool the people of God that our faith is so great, and yet we don't even have mustard seed faith.

This is a generation where everything is my way or no way. What if Jesus had said he did not want to heal you today or that He did not want to go to the cross for us? Where would your faith be then? I thank God that He did go to the cross.

## Faith That Works Through Love

We "front" love in the church, at home, and to the world. We act like we love people, and then we go behind their backs and talk about them. Sometimes I think we, the church, keep more "mess" going on with each other than the world does. Why can't we be like the Bible says in John 15:12, "…That ye love one another, as I have loved you." Just think for a moment. You're to love your neighbor, enemies, and friends as Christ loved us. If we loved like Christ loved, the devil would not be able to sow discord, malice, envy, or jealousy in our hearts. A lot of times we tell people that we love them with a fake smile on our face. We tell people we love them to get what we want from them. If you stop to think about it for a moment I know you can think of the times that you lied and said you loved someone but really did not want to be near that person much less have anything at all to do with them. Our love should be pure as God's love is for us.

## CRAZY FAITH

Faith in God will change the way you love people. The reason why I can say this is because when I first came into the real knowledge of Christ I learned what real love was. I thought love was buying gifts for everyone and making them happy regardless of how I felt. When someone wanted something, regardless if they needed it or not, I would try to get it for them because I always enjoyed seeing people happy and with smiles on their faces. Anyway, I know that with faith in God, He can turn your hate or distrust into love. What you thought you would never forgive, you will find yourself being healed of that hurt, which will result in love. No matter how you have been hurt in life, God can and will heal that hurt through your faith in Him.

There was someone in my life who I really loved, and she had been hurt by people and especially by some of her family members. She felt she could never forgive them because of the things that had transpired during her childhood. I was glad that the Lord allowed her to talk with me because God had done a healing in me with some past hurts. We talked about the Lord and how He had healed me. I had to let her know that if God did it for me that He would do the same for her. In life, when we have been hurt by the people we love and friends we trusted, we really do not want to trust anymore. We fear that the hurt will happen again. God gave me favor with this person because she normally does not want to listen to what anyone has to say regarding the Lord. She listened attentively and understood what I told her. I told her that God can wipe all the hurt away as He had done for me and fill her with love for everybody. When I wanted to love my enemies and the people that hurt me, I asked God to give me the kind of love (agape) that He had for us when He gave His Son for us. I want you to know that it did not happen over-night. My faith was not where it should have been. As my faith grew in God, it was awesome how love for people came in my life. Once we have learned how to forgive, God can fill our heart with love. Don't say you forgave someone and then continue to talk about the situation all the time. I'm not saying that you will never think about it, but you will not meditate on it to the point that you begin to hate. God can fill you with love if you really want to love people.

I thank God that we do not have to pretend. We don't have to pretend to love. Christ died for us. If we accept Him, we are who He says we are – heirs of God and joint heirs with Jesus Christ. We are the righteousness of God. (Romans 8:17, II Corinthians 5:21). That's something to be godly proud of. We are part – no, we **are the Royal Priesthood**. God has chosen us:

> But ye are a chosen generation, a royal priesthood, a holy nation, a peculiar people; that ye should shew forth the praises of Him who hath called you out of darkness into His marvelous light;
> Which in time past were not a people, but are now the people of God: which had not obtained mercy, but now have obtained mercy (I Peter 2: 9-10).

A songwriter once wrote, "Be true to who you are." If we have to pretend that we have all the faith to move mountains, why are we struggling? Why are we struggling with the pressures of life? I'm not saying that every day will be a bed of roses, but if we had the kind of faith that Christ says we should have, we will be able to speak to those mountains in our lives – mountains of debt and poverty, mountains of depression and oppression, mountains of marital unhappiness, mountains of despair and despondency, and mountains of whatever you're struggling with, and make them MOVE! We should be able to speak to them, and they obey us because of the Word that pours forth from our lips. The key is allowing God's Word to "dwell in us richly." (Colossians 3:16) We also have to continue praying and seeking His face for deliverance. God is good and stands able and willing to deliver us from our present distresses if we only come to

# CRAZY FAITH

Him in faith and believe He is able to do just what He said. A teenager from our church wrote these two poems:

## Being Real For Jesus
### (Part 1)

Who do you think you are coming **in this place**
trying to fool God's people with that mask on your face?
Just be yourself. Who are you trying to impress?
You don't have to get around the saints and act like you're the best.
Because as soon as the week comes you're back to your old way.
And you act like you don't care about that Word that was preached last Sunday.
When you get around your so-called friends you pull off this act.
And as soon as they're gone, you're talking about them behind their back.
Be real for Jesus because it will catch up with you.
And don't think you're getting away with it because he knows everything you do.
Being real for Jesus sometimes means giving up things you love,
Doing what's right and sacrificing for the one up above.
Bitterness, hate, gossip only brings you down low.
And now it has come a time to let these things go.
Concentrate on God, and don't worry what people say
Because it is not going to be them you'll stand before on judgment day.
Being real for Jesus sometimes it takes being by yourself.
but you've got to say as long as I've got Jesus Christ, I don't need nobody else.

Written by Quatia Craig

# Dr. Linda Smith

## Being Real For Jesus
### (Part 2)

Have you gone back to your old ways and put your mask back on?
Still doing things that you know are wrong?
Are you not yet ready for the next level?
Were you not able to hold that which God poured into your soul and became a leaky vessel?
So what will it take?
What are you holding on to?
At any moment we could slip into eternity, and the place that we end up is the place we choose.
God is sending similar messages year after year, and still we are not real.
But when will you **stand, make a change** and let your purpose here on earth fulfill?
The clock is ticking away, and time is winding down.
So now we must live in absolute obedience to him in order to hear that last sound
To board and depart and be on our way home.
And get into his presence without our mask on.
Pray and ask God to help you stand on your confession
And <u>always pray that your faith will not fail you in the time of testing</u>.
Sometimes it will not be easy, but it will always be well,
So what is the choice of your destination now...
**Heaven or Hell?**

Written by Quatia Craig

## Crazy Faith

When there is no way
What am I going to do?
Where will I turn? Who will I turn to?
When I struggle every day and barely get by,
I'm looking for answers and asking God why.
So many things hitting me left and right,
Getting stressed for no reason, losing sleep at night.
But, where is the faith that I thought I had,
The kind that I needed when things got bad?
The kind that I always ask God for
When I knew he'll make a way when there aren't any more.
When my money is low and my payments are behind,
I will trust and believe they will get paid on time.
When I am hungry and I have nothing to eat,
I will trust and believe God will come through for me.
When everything that I have has been traded for sorrow,
I will trust and believe I will get it back tomorrow.
When I am sick to my body and it just doesn't seem real,
I will trust and believe by His stripes I am healed.
This is the kind of faith no one understands.
It is beyond the imagination of every man.
This is the kind of faith that you hold on to
No matter whatever you may go through.
When danger is around and you feel safe
Just thank God…
For your
Crazy Faith.

Written by Quatia Craig

It should be our prayer that the Lord will give His people discernment to know when other members of the body, not just our local assemblies, but the body, are fronting — saying great, swelling words but inwardly are crying out for help. And when the Lord reveals those that need help, we will not act like we have got it all together, but we will go to them in love and with compassion and pull them up out of their pits.

# 15

## Are We Exercising Faith?

I read a book called <u>Faith, Foolishness or Presumption,</u> by Dr. Fredrick Price and the title is what caught my attention. In life we have a tendency to act foolishly and always presume something and yet we say we have faith. Dr. Price says, "Faith must be a way of life." In the Word of God it says, "The just shall live by faith." (Habakkuk 2:4; Romans 1:17, Galatians 3:11) Who are the just? The just are the righteous. The Message Translation says:

> I want you to know, my very dear friends that it is on account of this resurrected Jesus that the forgiveness of your sins can be promised.
> He accomplishes, in those who believe, everything that the Law of Moses could never make good on. But everyone who believes in this raised-up Jesus is declared good and right and whole before God (Acts 13:38-39 MSG).

Regarding righteousness:

> Look at the proud; his soul is not straight or right within him, but the [rigidly] just and the

[uncompromisingly] righteous man shall live by his faith and in his faithfulness (Habakkuk 2:4 AMP).

If we are righteous, then we should live by the Word of God. For those who are not righteous, the Bible says in Hebrews 10:38-39 (NASB):

But my righteous one shall live by faith; and if he shrinks back, my soul has no pleasure in him. But we are not of those who shrink back to destruction, but of those who have faith to the preserving of the soul.

I definitely do not want to be one of those who pull back from God. God will have no pleasure, or can I say, He will not be pleased with us if we pull back. I really want to please God and the Word of God says, "But without faith it is impossible to please him..." (Hebrews 11:6). Some of us say with our mouths that we want to please God, but our hearts are somewhere else. This walk in Christ is by faith. Again, II Corinthians 5:7 says, "For we walk by faith, not by sight." This means, I'm not going by what I see or what I can do, but that I will trust God in whatever He tells me to do.

We say we are walking by faith. Does that mean we go to God with every little thing? No, but I Thessalonians 5:17 says, "Pray without ceasing." In other words, any decision that needs to be made, we should pray and let God direct our path. I can say that I have not always walked by faith but that I have let my emotions (feelings) and what I think I know take precedence over the Word of God. If I do not read His word then I cannot receive all the benefits that come from walking with Christ.

# Dr. Linda Smith

## Presumption

How many times have we presumed that God would do a particular thing? Some have said they were walking in faith. When what they thought should have come to pass did not take place, was this faith or presumption?

To presume means "to take something for granted; to assume" (Webster's New World Dictionary and Thesaurus). If we do not act on the Word, we fall into presumption. Faith always has a corresponding action. If I have faith to be healed of diabetes, I will not continue to eat everything in sight and never exercise. That's presumption. If I have faith that God will bless me with a job, I will not lie in bed until 11:00 a.m. and never fill out an application. That's presumption. Both examples were presumption. Faith acts on the Word of God. James 2:15-17 says:

> If a brother or sister be naked and destitute of daily food,
> And one of you say unto them, Depart in peace, be ye warmed and filled; notwithstanding ye give them not those things which are needful to the body; what doth it profit?
> Even so faith, if it hath not works, is dead, being alone.

We must act on what the Word says regarding each petition that we place at His feet.

Once we have found what God's Word says regarding our petition, we are to stand on that, meditate on that, speak that, and believe that. Our actions should reflect what we are speaking.

I have a relative that loves God. She had been struggling financially and was believing God to bring her out. The Lord let her know that He was going to bless her financially and bless her with another job. Before the Lord spoke this to her, someone presented her with an opportunity, and she was prayerfully considering it. Well, when the Lord had told her He would bless her, she began making preparations to accept this opportunity. The Lord never told her how He would do it or when, but that He would. Soon, other opportunities crossed her path, and she failed to act on them because she had this first opportunity stuck in her mind. Things did not work out the way she planned because she was waiting for the first opportunity to come to fruition. She now believes that those other opportunities were stepping stones to the first opportunity. She really believes that the first opportunity was where God was leading, but God had a plan in place that was going to take time. Valuable time and resources had been lost because she presumed God would do it a particular way.

We must stay in God's Word for His direction for our lives and stay in tune with His voice to hear from Him. After she realized her error, she revisited what God had promised and listened and waited on Him for His guidance. The Lord has blessed her beyond what she could have imagined, but she had to learn to listen and to wait.

## The Body of Christ

In the body of Christ everyone is given a measure of faith. We may all start out with the same amount of faith, but it depends on you if you remain the same or if you grow. The apostles in Mark 17:5 asked the Lord to "Increase our faith." So, if their faith had to be increased, so does ours. Did you notice how Jesus responded to their request? It almost sounds like He "changed the subject," but He did not. He said, "If you had faith as a grain of mustard seed, you might say..." In effect, He was saying, if you want faith's action to increase in your life, you must plant your faith as seed. How do you plant it? By <u>saying</u>. You "say" unto the mountain. You "say" unto the problem. Using your faith is like using a muscle. The more you use it, the more it grows or is strengthened. Jesus was answering their request, just not in the way they expected. He was telling them that the way to increase the effect of their faith in life and circumstances is to use their faith by saying what they believe and refusing to come off of that stand. Simply praying, "Lord increase my faith," doesn't cause it to grow. Jesus did not rebuke them for making the request, but He gently redirected them to what they really should do to cause their faith to get stronger. He told them to use it!

How can we expect God to move mountains for us if we don't grow in His Word? The body of Christ wants God to do everything for them but don't want to do what it takes for their faith to increase. Dr. Price says, "Every person who accepts Christ as his or her personal Savior has faith. Faith is a requirement of salvation." (Price, <u>Faith, Foolishness, or Presumption</u>). It's up to you to develop it.

> For it is by free grace (God's unmerited favor) that you are saved (delivered from judgment and made partakers of Christ's salvation) through [your] faith. And this [salvation] is not of yourselves [of your own doing, it came not through Your own striving], but it is the gift of God (Ephesians 2:8 AMP).

"Faith cometh by hearing, and hearing by the word of God." (Romans 10:17) If we do not hear the Word of God, how can our faith grow? Another perquisite for our faith to grow is, we must attend a church where the true Word of God is being preached. By attending a church where the Word is being preached our spiritual body is being fed and nourished. This causes growth and maturity to come to our spirits. God's Word also says that we should not forsake the assembly of one another. We never know when God shares something that will be beneficial to someone else. We should never hold back or keep to ourselves what God has given to be shared with others. Their lives need that nourishment, also. God blesses us so that we can go out and bless others. We should never be selfish when it comes to sharing the Word with others.

# 16

## Hindrances of Faith

Hindrance means "the act of hindering, any person or thing that hinders; obstacle; impediment; obstruction" (<u>Webster's New World Dictionary and Thesaurus</u>). Faith means unquestioning belief that does not require proof or evidence, unquestioning belief in God, religious tenets, complete trust, confidence, or reliance." (Ibid.)

Dr. Price talked about five things that spoil the vine as in Song of Solomon 2:15, "Take us the foxes, the little foxes, that spoil the vines: for our vines *have* tender grapes." When we say one thing and live another, we spoil the vines. Dr. Price gave five things that "spoil the vines." I would like to add some others.

I want to call this The Hindrances of Our Faith because it stops us from believing God. It stops us from trusting God because we put our trust in man. Psalms 118 says, "It *is* better to trust in the LORD than to put confidence in man." Man will fail us, but God will never fail us.

The five foxes that Dr. Price spoke about in his book, <u>Five Little Foxes of Faith</u> are:

1. Unforgiveness – A Snare for Our Faith

2. Worry – The Sin of Not Trusting God

3. Fear – A Robbing Spirit

4. The Battle of the Mind

5. Losing Hope

My list would include the entire list above, plus:

1. Our mouths and how we kill one another

2. Our attitudes and how nasty we are

## Unforgiveness

We must learn how to forgive one another as Christ forgives us. How can we expect God to forgive us of our sins if we cannot forgive our sisters and brothers? In Mark 11:25-26 it says:

> And when ye stand praying, forgive, if ye have ought against any: that your Father also which is in heaven may forgive you your trespasses.
> But if ye do not forgive, neither will your Father which is in heaven forgive your trespasses.

Unforgiveness in our hearts can hinder us from having faith.

If you read Mark 11:22-26 you will understand what I'm saying:

> And Jesus answering saith unto them, Have faith in God.
> For verily I say unto you, That whosoever shall say unto this mountain, Be thou removed, and be thou cast into the sea; and shall not doubt in his heart, but shall believe that those things which he saith shall come to pass; he shall have whatsoever he saith.
> Therefore I say unto you, What things soever ye desire, when ye pray, believe that ye receive them, and ye shall have them.
> And when ye stand praying, forgive, if ye have ought against any: that your Father also which is in heaven may forgive you your trespasses.
> But if ye do not forgive, neither will your Father which is in heaven forgive your trespasses.

Notice the word "and" in verse 25. "And" is a conjunction; it connects other words or phrases. And when ye stand praying, forgive,…". In the previous verses Jesus talked about having faith, speaking to the mountains in our lives and receiving our request. But, then He connects forgiving. We can reason then that forgiveness is a prerequisite (a necessary condition) to asking and receiving.

I mentioned the case with the young lady who had problems with forgiving those who had hurt her. During that particular time when both of us discussed forgiveness she was not saved. Today, she is saved and has found a place of forgiveness – not only for herself – but she has learned to forgive others. Christ had to remove the hurt and cleanse her heart before she could see clearly. If she continued to harbor ill feelings, she could not find a place of forgiveness for herself. Verse 26 says, "But if ye do not forgive, neither will your Father which is in heaven forgive your trespasses."

To prove this point, let's look at Matthew 18:21-35. These

verses tell about the servant who owed the king ten-thousand talents. When he could not pay, the king ordered him, his wife and children and all his personal possessions to be sold. Well, the servant fell down and begged the king to just give him some time, and he would pay the debt in full. The king felt that this man's plea was genuine. He felt sorry for the servant and decided he would do more than give him time to pay, he would totally release him from the debt. Can you imagine being released from your creditors, not because you paid what you owed, but because they decided to erase the debt? Let's say you purchased a home for one hundred thousand dollars. After some time has passed you get a letter in the mail that says, "Your loan has been paid in full. Please do not send any payments." Your heart would probably skip a beat! You would probably run through your house exclaiming you could not believe it!

Instead of being eternally grateful, this servant found someone that owed him a little money and when that person could not pay him, he became angry and grabbed the man by the throat. Of course, the man pleaded for mercy, but he was unrelenting. He had the man thrown into prison until the debt was paid. Well, when the king found out what happened, he became angry. The king thought this servant who was forgiven of the debt should have had mercy on his fellow servant. So the king reversed his previous decision and had him jailed until he could pay his debt. Verse 35 says, "So likewise shall my heavenly Father do also unto you if ye from your hearts forgive not every one his brother their trespasses."

## Worry

We should not have to discuss this topic. Worry means to be anxious. Philippians 4:6 says, "Do not be anxious about anything, but in everything by prayer and petition, with thanksgiving, present your requests to God" (NIV). Simply put, this verse means that we should not worry about anything. Why? Because part "B" says we are praying and petitioning God who understands all things. The result of praying to God with full assurance that He can and will work for you is in verse 7: "And the peace of God, which transcends all understanding, will guard your hearts and your minds in Christ Jesus" (NIV). So, if we are placing our request at the Master's feet, we can leave them there knowing he will take care of the rest. He already knows what we need before we even ask. The scriptures tell us not to worry about tomorrow (or about anything else):

> Wherefore, if God so clothe the grass of the field, which today is, and tomorrow is cast into the oven, shall he not much more clothe you, O ye of little faith?
> Therefore take no thought, saying, What shall we eat? or, What shall we drink? or, Wherewithal shall we be clothed?
> (For after all these things do the Gentiles seek:) for your heavenly Father knoweth that ye have need of all these things.
> But seek ye first the kingdom of God, and his righteousness; and all these things shall be added unto you.
> Take therefore no thought for the morrow: for the morrow shall take thought for the things of itself. Sufficient unto the day *is* the evil thereof. (Matthew 6:30-34)

## Fear

Fear is "anxiety [worry] caused by real or possible danger or to be afraid of; terror; panic; doubt" (Webster's New World Dictionary and Thesaurus). Look at the first definition for fear. It is anxiety or worry. We just talked about worry. II Timothy 1:7 says, "For God has not given us the spirit of fear, but of power and of love and of a sound mind." I John 4:18 says, "... but perfect love casteth out fear: because fear hath torment. He that feareth is made perfect in love." Fear and worry seem to work together. First there is worry, then fear sets in. Fear can grip you and cause you to lose control. Price points out that the scripture says fear is a spirit. If fear is not of God, then the spirit is from Satan.

Dr. Price calls fear "a robbing spirit" (Price, Five Little Foxes of Faith).

Dr. Price also points out that there is a difference between respect and fear:

> ...you may say, "I am afraid of fire,"...I have fire in my water heater, fire cooks my food. But there is no way I will stick my hand into a fire, because I know that fire burns. So even though I am not afraid of fire, I do have a respect for it... Here is how you can tell when a spirit of fear is dominating you. When whatever it is you are afraid of causes you to panic or become paralyzed with fright, that is a spirit of fear in action" (Ibid. 27-28).

We can agree with those statements because the Word says that there is torment in fear (I John 4:18). Fear and faith cannot exist together. When Peter got out of the ship and began walking to Jesus, he was fine until he lost focus, and then fear set in: "But when he saw the wind boisterous, he was afraid; and beginning to sink, he cried saying, Lord, save me" (Matthew 14:30). When fear came in, faith left. It is just like oil and water. They don't mix!

Did you know that the fearful have no part in heaven?

> But the <u>fearful</u>, and unbelieving, and the abominable, and murderers, and whoremongers, and sorcerers, and idolators, all liars, shall have their part in the lake which burneth with fire and brimstone: which is the second death (Revelation 21:8).

The fearful are lumped together with liars and whoremongers! Don't get mad! I'm just the messenger! We must exercise our authority over this spirit of fear, bind it, and cast it out, according to God's Word, and live in peace (God's peace) and victory. Where God's Word is, there is peace. Saturate, as we have said over and over again, your mind with God's Word so there will be no room for fear.

## The Battle of the Mind

The mind is probably where Christians battle the enemy the most. Why does Satan battle us so? He's after our faith. He wants to destroy the trust and the confidence that we have in God. He does that by planting things in our minds against God, against ourselves, against other believers, against our families and friends. And he will use the things that we've talked about such as fear, unforgiveness, and worry. But when he comes at us with negative thoughts we have to counter-attack with the Word. The only way to defeat the enemy in the battle of the mind is to know the Word and to use the Word of God effectively with our faith.

II Corinthians 10:4-5 says:

> (For the weapons of our warfare *are* not carnal, but mighty through God to the pulling down of strong holds;)
> Casting down imaginations, and every high thing that exalteth itself against the knowledge of God, and bringing into captivity every thought to the obedience of Christ...

The Bible calls Satan the "god of this world." (II Corinthians 4:4) If he is allowed to wreak havoc in our minds, he can destroy us spiritually which will lead to our ultimate destruction. If he is victorious in our minds, he will blind us to the truths in God's Word and eventually destroy our faith. II Corinthians 4:4 says:

> In whom the god of this world hath blinded the minds of them which believe not, lest the light of the glorious gospel of Christ, who is the image of God, should shine unto them.

Jesus Himself had to battle the enemy. The devil attacked the Lord Jesus when He was most vulnerable. In Matthew 4, Jesus had fasted for forty days and forty nights. After this, Jesus was hungry, and Satan spoke to Him and said, "...If Thou be the Son of God, command that these stones be made bread" (Matthew 4:3). What did we say the counter-attack had to be? This was Jesus' reply: "It is written, Man shall not live by bread alone, but by every Word that proceedeth out of the mouth of God" (Matthew 4:4). He counter-attacked with the Word! It is so important to know that we are no match for the devil apart from God's Word.

## Dr. Linda Smith

John 1:1 states, "In the beginning was the Word, and the Word was with God, and the Word was God." Is not that awesome – the Word (Jesus) counter-attacked with the Word!

Each time the enemy launched his assault against Jesus' mind with "If", Christ countered with, "It is written…"

> Then the devil taketh him up into the holy city, and setteth him on a pinnacle of the temple.
> And saith unto him, If thou be the Son of God, cast thyself down: for it is written, He shall give his angels charge concerning thee: and in their hands they shall bear thee up, lest at any time thou dash thy foot against a stone.
> Jesus said unto him, It is written again, Thou shalt not tempt the Lord thy God.
> Again, the devil taketh him up into an exceeding high mountain, and showeth him all the kingdoms of the world, and the glory of them;
> And saith unto him, All these things will I give thee, if thou wilt fall down and worship me.
> Then saith Jesus unto him, Get thee hence, Satan: for it is written, Thou shalt worship the Lord thy God, and him only shalt thou serve (Matthew 4:5-10).

And guess what happened next? Verse 11 says, "Then the devil <u>leaveth</u> Him, and, behold, angels came and ministered unto Him." That's right! He, Satan, was defeated. Jesus cast the devil's thoughts down without hesitation and did not entertain them. We must do the same when Satan launches an attack against us. We must use the Word against him and watch him flee. This does not mean that he will not return, but he will leave after a whipping from the Word!

We determine the condition of our minds. If we have read

and meditated on God's Word like we should, we can defeat the enemy. If you have no time for study and prayer and spending time in God's presence, you will constantly be defeated and have no direction for your life. If you keep your mind on God, He will keep you in perfect peace (Isaiah 26:3).

## **Losing Hope**

Hope is the essence of faith. These two work together. Hope keeps you focused until the promise is received and faith gets the job done. It brings the promise into reality. I like what Dr. Price said:

> Before I learned to walk by faith, all my wife and I lived on was hope. Hope did not do anything to change my circumstances, just as it will not change what happens in your life. Faith is what releases the power of God to change your life; hope will simply keep you alive until things change (Price, <u>Five Little Foxes of Faith</u>).

We must not lose heart in our walk. There will be times of testing and trial, but if we continue to hold onto God's promises we can be victorious. There have been tests that I have failed, and there have been times when I was down. But the point is I had hope. I did not have to stay discouraged because things did not work the way I wanted them to work. At some point I had to pick myself up, dust myself off, and try it again. Jonas Salk, the man who created the polio vaccine tried two hundred times before he came up with the right mixture. He did not view it as two hundred failures but as "two hundred ways how not to vaccinate for polio" (Ortberg, <u>If You Want to Walk on Water, You've Got to Get Out of the Boat</u>).

II Corinthians 4:8-9 says:

> We are troubled on every side, yet not distressed; we are perplexed, but not in despair; Persecuted, but not forsaken; cast down, but not destroyed…

There will be times of discouragement, but we must not lose hope. No matter what we are facing we should know that we are more than conquerors through Him that loved us (Romans 8:37).

## Attitude

Did you know that it is not always what we go through but how we go through something that determines whether or not we were victorious?

What you think about helps to create your attitude. It is important to think on the right things so that our attitudes can be right. Philippians 4:8 says:

> Finally, brethren, whatsoever things are true, whatsoever things are honest, whatsoever things are just, whatsoever things are pure, whatsoever things are lovely, whatsoever things are of good report; if there be any virtue, and if there be any praise, think on these things.

If we fill our minds with the lovely, just, honest, true, etc., when we open our mouths to speak, only what is lovely, just, honest, true, etc., will come out. This will also be seen in our attitude and the way we carry ourselves. John Ortberg wrote:

> The way you think creates your attitudes; the way you think shapes your emotions; the way you think governs your behavior, the way you think deeply influences your immune system and vulnerability to illness. Everything about you flows out of the way you think. (Ortberg, <u>If You Want to Walk on Water, You've Got to Get Out of the Boat</u>).

Whatever goes in comes out. If we put junk in, junk will come out:

> Your mind will think most about what it is exposed to. What repeatedly enters your mind occupies your mind, eventually shapes your mind, and will ultimately express itself in what you do and who you become...People are surprised that what their minds are constantly exposed to, attend to, and dwell on eventually comes out in how they feel and what they do (Ibid).

God's Word is lovely, just, honest, true, etc. It is all those things found in Philippians 4:8. So again, we must saturate our minds with God's Word in order to have a positive attitude.

I mentioned that it is <u>how</u> we go through that is important. When tests and trials come our way, God not only looks for obedience but willingness. Isaiah 1:19 says, "If ye be willing and obedient, ye shall eat the good of the land." Notice the conjunction "and"? The verse after that says, "But if ye refuse and rebel, ye shall be devoured with the sword: for the mouth of the Lord hath spoken it" (Isaiah 1:20).

I have heard people say, "If you are obedient you'll eat the good of the land!" They seem to always leave out the "willing" part. Abraham had to be <u>willing</u> to give his son. Jesus had to be

<u>willing</u> to give His life. When you ask your children to do something such as, "Johnny, take out the trash," if Johnny mumbles something underneath his breath, do we say, "Oh, Johnny, you're such a sweet and obedient child?" No, I would think not! You would probably swing your head around and say, "What did you say?!" We do not get joy out of it when our children do things grudgingly. The same holds true with God. Paul wrote about giving:

> Every man according as he purposeth in his heart, so let him give; not grudgingly, or of necessity: for God loveth a cheerful giver.

A willing attitude is pliable. We do not want to have a "goat" mentality, but we want to pliable in the Master's hand.

I believe when we fail to have a positive attitude in test or trials, we may have to repeat that test again. When we fail a test, the instructor will sometimes make us re-take the test. If we are going through the same tests over and over again, maybe we need to stop and examine what is taking place. Ask God why you seem to be going in circles. We may find the answer in our attitude.

## The Power of the Tongue

The tongue is a powerful muscle. It can destroy, and it can create life. It can build up, and it can tear down. The Bible says **no one** is able to tame the tongue. (This means no one in their own natural ability.) Through God, thankfully, we can train our tongue through His power! That's why David prayed, in Psalms 141:3, "Set a watch, O LORD, before my mouth; keep, the door of my lips." Remember, we said if all we are putting in our minds and spirits is junk, that's what will spill forth from our mouth. That's why it is so important that we nourish ourselves (our spirits) with the Word. Marilyn Hickey states:

> Our faith will rise and fall on the word we speak. For this reason, it is vitally important that we learn to speak fluently the language of faith (Hickey, Marilyn, WOW Faith).

The world was created by God speaking the Word, "And God said, Let there be... and it was so" (Genesis 1:14-15). He has also given us that creative power.

Mark 11:23 says:

> For verily I say unto you, That whosoever shall say unto this mountain, Be thou removed, and be thou cast into the sea; and shall not doubt in his heart, but shall believe that those things which he saith shall come to pass; he shall have whatsoever he saith.

God made us just like Himself. We were created after His image and after His likeness (Genesis 1:26-27). If God can "give life to the dead and calls into being that which does not exist," so can we! (Romans 4:17 NAS). Jesse Duplantis, a great man of faith, once said that man is a "speaking spirit," and a spirit is the only one that can destroy the earth because God gave him dominion of the earth. He states that God made man like Himself, and when God blew life in his nostrils man became a "speaking-spirit," able to create by speaking. That is a powerful thought! All the more reason why we have to watch what comes out of our mouths. Our words can either defeat us or guide us to victory. The latter part of Matthew 12:34 says, "... out of the abundance of the heart, the mouth speaketh." Hickey agrees:

The words we speak begin as thoughts in our minds. Our hearts shape the way we think and feel, and those thoughts and feelings come out in our words (Hickey, Marilyn, <u>WOW Faith</u>).

Sometimes we say negative things such as, "We gonna leave this world with something," meaning some type of sickness or disease; "That child is gonna be the death of me," or "I just cannot take it anymore." Those things will eventually happen if we keep confessing them. The Scripture says you shall have whatever you say (Mark 11:23). We need to change our confessions to positive ones. I know we don't mean some things literally, but we have to realize that there is creative power in our tongues, and God will judge everything that we have spoken:

> But I say unto you, That every idle word that men shall speak, they shall give account thereof in the day of judgment.
> For by thy words thou shalt be justified, and by thy words thou shalt be condemned (Matthew 12:36-37).

## Murmuring and Complaining

Murmuring and complaining gets us in trouble also. Some of the children of Israel were destroyed because they murmured and complained. Numbers 14:27-37 reads:

> How long shall I bear with this evil congregation, which murmur against me? I have heard the murmurings of the children of Israel, which they murmur against me.
> Say unto them, As truly as I live, saith the Lord, as

ye have spoken in mine ears, so will I do to you:
Your carcases shall fall in this wilderness; and all that were numbered of you, according to your whole number, from twenty years old and upward, which have murmured against me,
Doubtless ye shall not come into the land, concerning which I sware to make you dwell therein, save Caleb the son Jephunneh, and Joshua the son of Nun.
But you little ones, which ye said should be a prey, them will I bring in, and they shall know the land which ye have despised.
But as for you, your carcases, they shall fall in this wilderness.
And your children shall wander in the wilderness forty years, and bear your whoredoms, until your carcases be wasted in the wilderness.
After the number of the days in which ye searched the land, even forty days, each day for a year, shall ye bear your iniquities, even forty years, and ye shall know my breach of promise.
I the Lord have said, I will surely do it unto all this evil congregation, that are gathered together against me: in this wilderness they shall be consumed, and there they shall die.
And the men, which Moses sent to search the land, who returned, and made all the congregation to murmur against him, by bringing up slander upon the land.
Even those men that did bring up the evil report upon the land, died by the plague before the Lord.

The Israelites, though they were God's chosen people, were constant complainers. Instead of trusting God to provide and deliver them from the wilderness they would complain to Moses about what they did or did not have, what they could or could not do. Moses would go to God with their complaint, and God would perform a miracle to get them what they needed. But as soon as that blessing was out of sight and out of mind, they would complain about something else. They even complained about the blessings!

Today, God's people are still the same way. We murmur and complain about what we **don't** have instead of thanking God for what we **do** have. As soon as a crisis arises we fail to remember what the Lord has already done for us and begin to complain. My pastor preached a message once entitled, "People Are So Easy to Forget What God Has Done for Them." Is not that so true? Before the next crisis arrives, it is our job to fill ourselves up on God's Word. If the Word dwelt in us richly we would find less and less to complain about.

God is looking for faith – **Bible Faith** – that will believe and trust Him no matter what outside circumstances dictate. He wants to hear faith coming from our lips. I'm not saying that we should never express to God how we feel regarding certain situations or circumstances. But when we place our petition with God it should be followed immediately by praise and thanksgiving. Again, Philippians 4:6 says, "Be careful for nothing; but in everything by prayer and supplication **with** thanksgiving let your requests be made known unto God." We were created to give God glory. He deserves to hear praise coming out of these earthen vessels. Murmuring does not bring Him glory; neither does complaining change our circumstances.

## Gossip

There is another subject that falls under "The Power of the Tongue". That subject is gossip. You may ask, "What does gossip have to do with faith?" Don't forget. We are talking about what hinders faith. Because both sweet water and bitter water cannot flow out of the same place, gossip has to be bitter water flowing from a corrupt fountain. Hickey agrees and writes:

> Just as a diseased tree will produce bad fruit, so a corrupt heart will produce evil thoughts, words, and actions. On the other hand, a pure heart, like a healthy tree, will bring forth pure and healthy fruit: **strong faith**, wise and helpful words, and positive behavior. (Hickey, WOW Faith).

That's why we are discussing gossip. If our tree is healthy, there would be pure thoughts. Pure thoughts do not produce gossip. A healthy tree produces strong faith because of the nourishment that the tree is getting. This nourishment would have to include healthy doses of the Word, prayer, fastings, and fellowship with others. A healthy tree does not slander its brother or sister.

How many people have we murdered with our tongues? What do I mean? When we defame someone's character before someone else, we are killing their influence. We are destroying that person's character and reputation.

> These six things doth the Lord hate: yea, seven are an abomination unto Him
> ...hands that shed innocent blood
> ...and he that soweth discord among brethren.
> (Proverbs 6:16, 17, 19).

Sowing discord is an abomination to God. An abomination is something that is abhorred or detested by God. Abomination is an extreme hatred. God hates gossip or anything that would cause dissension among brothers and sisters. If God hates it, we should hate it, too.

## Dr. Linda Smith

Self-control begins with our tongue. Careless words do incredible harm, and once spoken, are impossible to recall...One of the most dangerous kinds of careless words is gossip. Gossip can destroy not only the life and reputation of the person being talked about, but also those of the person doing the talking as well...Whether or not those "facts" are true is of no concern. For this reason, someone who spreads gossip reveals a basic lack of integrity (Hickey, WOW FAITH).

# 17

## A Character Study of Faith

## Ruth

The Book of Ruth portrays a family that was faithful in honoring God and pictures divine providence even in the mist of adversities and sorrow. Even when we are going through a storm, we sometimes are not faithful in honoring God the way this family did. We should honor God and give Him praise during bad times **and** when we are happy and receiving the blessings of God. Most of the time we sit around and complain about what is happening in our lives and wondering if God will really bring us out. Then we find ourselves saying things that are contrary to His Word such as, "If God sees fit to get me out of this" or "If it is His will…" We need to get rid of those two letters – "I", "F" – when it comes to God because we know that He **can and will** do what He has promised when we **trust Him.**

The story of Ruth takes place in Moab with the death of Naomi's husband. Subsequently, her married sons would die and Naomi would be left with her two daughters-in-law.

## Ruth's Character – The Ideal Daughter-In-Law

Ruth is a devoted daughter-in-law. Naomi, seeing that her husband and children are dead, decides to return to her homeland, Judah. She insists that the two young ladies return to their homeland also, but Ruth refuses to leave her. Ruth was a true friend to Naomi. She exemplified what her name meant – friend. How many daughters-in-law can say that they truly love their mothers-in-law as Ruth did? Today we hear more daughters-in-law complain about their in-laws instead of loving them unconditionally. They complain to their husbands, but we should put ourselves in that spouse's shoes and know that the other person feels bad after their parent has been criticized. Some mothers-in-law may be guilty of every complaint, but we should consider our spouses' feelings. I thank God that I had wonderful and loving in-laws. They have gone on to be with the Lord, but while they were living, I gave God praise for them. I can truly say that I loved them unconditionally. God placed a special love in me for my in-laws before my husband and I were married.

Ruth was unselfish and committed to her mother-in-law. She loved Naomi so much that she was willing to follow her no matter what:

> Then she arose with her daughters-in-law, that she might return from the country of Moab: for she had heard in the country of Moab how that the Lord had visited His people in giving them bread.
> Wherefore she went forth out of the place where she was, and her two daughters-in-law with her; and they went on their way to return unto the land of Judah.
> And Naomi said unto her two daughters-in-law, Go, return each to her mother's house: the Lord

deal kindly with you, as you have dealt with the dead, and with me (Ruth 1:6-8).

Through Ruth's tender and loving care, God brought comfort to Naomi in her greatest hurt following the deaths of her husband and sons:

> And Ruth said, Entreat me not leave thee, or to return from following After thee: for whither thou goest, I will go; and where thou lodgest, I will lodge; thy people shall be my people, and thy God my God:
> Where thou diest, will I die, and there will I be buried: the Lord do so to me, and more also, if aught but death part thee and me.
> When she saw that she was steadfastly minded to go with her, then she left speaking unto her (Ruth 1:16-18).

Ruth's commitment to her inheritance was real. We need to be committed to Christ as Ruth was to Naomi. We seem to only want to commit when it benefits us. She had every right to walk away like Orpah, but Ruth counted the cost and made up her mind. Luke 14:27-32 says:

> And whosoever doth not bear his cross, and come after me, cannot be my disciple.
> For which of you, intending to build a tower, sitteth not down first, and counteth the cost, whether he have sufficient to finish it?
> Lest haply, after he hath laid the foundation, and is not able to finish it, all that behold it begin to mock him,
> Saying, This man began to build, and was not able to finish.
> Or what king, going to make war against another

> king sitteth not down first, and consulteth whether he be able with ten thousand to meet him that cometh against him with twenty thousand?
> Or else, while the other is yet a great way off, he sendeth an ambassage, and desireth conditions of peace.

Have you made a commitment to continue in your inheritance in Christ? Will you serve the Lord, no matter what?

Ruth was also Naomi's means of support. Each family usually had sufficient women to care for the complete needs of the household. There was no work for a woman outside of the home. The poor and the widow would have been destitute indeed, if God had not provided for them:

> And when ye reap the harvest of your land, thou shalt not wholly reap the corners of thy field, neither shalt thou gather the gleanings of thy harvest.
> And thou shalt not glean thy vineyard, neither shalt thou gather every grape of thy vineyard; thou shalt leave them for the poor and stranger: I am the Lord your God (Leviticus 19:9-10).

To be a gleaner with the other poor was a humbling task. Ruth was not afraid of hard work:

> And she said, I pray you, let me glean and gather after the reapers among the sheaves: so she came, and hath continued even from the morning until now, that she tarried a little in the house (Ruth 2:7).

She gleaned from the break of day until sun went down. After beating the grain from the stalks, she went home to Naomi. How many of us would work that hard for someone who was not even related by blood?

## Ruth Represents Every Believer

Ruth represents every believer today in that she was redeemed. When Boaz spread his skirt over Ruth, it was a symbolic pledge of marriage. She was the widow of Boaz's relative. Boaz could take her in because he could perform the "near kinsman" duty. And that's what Christ did for us. We were not God's chosen people. But He "spread His skirt" over us. I like the way Ezekiel put it:

> Now when I passed by thee, and looked upon thee, behold, thy time was the time of love; and **I spread my skirt over thee,** and covered thy nakedness: yea, I sware unto thee, and entered in a convenant with thee, saith the Lord God, and thou becamest mine.
> Then washed I thee with water; yea, I thoroughly washed away thy blood from thee, and I anointed thee with oil.
> I clothed thee also with embroidered work, and shod thee with badgers' skin, and I girded thee about with fine linen, and I covered thee with silk.
> I decked thee also with ornaments, and I put bracelets upon thy hands and a chain on thy neck.
> And I put a jewel on thy forehead, and earrings in thine ears, and a beautiful crown upon thine head (Ezekiel 16:8-12).

That is the description of the awesome power of God at redemption! Christ saw us polluted in our own blood – we were born in sin and shaped in iniquity! But Christ redeemed us. He thoroughly washed us and made us new creatures. Now we are clothed with fine linen – His righteousness! We have been grafted in. We were not a people but God has made us His people by the blood of Christ! Christ is our Kinsman Redeemer!

Ruth also serves as an example to Christian women everywhere because she possessed such virtues as "godliness, purity, humility, honesty, fidelity, and thoughtfulness." (The King James Study Bible) Also, Boaz serves as an example for Christian men because he was "a model of God-given strength, honor, graciousness, courtesy, and compassion" (Ibid.)

# 18

## CONCLUSION

We have shared so much about faith and what it means. We have shared examples of Bible faith – "crazy faith" in action. If we believe God's Word we know that things will get worse before they get better. The body of Christ will have to trust in God as never before. We will have to have crazy faith in order to stand against the wiles of the devil. Natural disasters. Are they really natural? Distress among the nations, turmoil in our homes and in our communities, job layoffs, the pressures of this life - all will demand faith from the people of God. The world will need someone to turn to. We have the answer, but are we walking in the faith of the Bible? Are **we** struggling with whether to believe God or to believe the enemy that says, "If thou be…"? The choice is yours.

We must allow our faith to grow to maturity. God does not want us to continue to be babes in Christ. We should not be tossed to and fro in our faith. It is our duty to reach a place in God that our faith will not be shaken. The storms of life will come, and winds will blow, but we must know in whom we believe. I believe that there is coming a time that the body of Christ will be tested, not only abroad but here, in our homeland. I believe Satan is coming for our very faith. Yes, we have had our own trials and tribulations but I believe our faith will be tested to the core. God will not allow His people to perish. He will provide the way of escape for us, but we must follow His lead.

Where does your faith stand? Do you want God to take your faith to another level, or are you comfortable where you are? Let's all endeavor to be what God has called us to be – kings and priests on this earth. Revelation 5:10 says, "And hast made us unto our God kings and priests: and we shall reign on the earth."

Let's all seek God and ask Him as the disciples did to increase our faith. Once you ask Him, be prepared for what you must do. Be prepared for the sacrifices you must make. Be prepared to spend time in the Word. Be prepared for required fasting and praying and laying aside every weight and sin to run this race (Hebrews 12:1). Be prepared to present your bodies as "living sacrifices, holy, acceptable unto God, which is our reasonable service" (Romans 12:1). Then WE will be prepared for that CRAZY FAITH!

# BIBLIOGRAPHY

Betters, Chuck and Sharon. Treasures of Faith. Phillipsburg, New Jersey: P&R Publishing Company 1999.

Bosworth, F.F. Christ The Healer. Grand Rapids, Michigan: Fleming H. Revell, 1973.

Copeland, Gloria. Blessed Beyond Measure. Tulsa, Oklahoma: Harrison House, Inc., 2004.

Easton's Bible Dictionary www.htmlbible.com/KJV30/easton/east3429.htm

Geisler, Norman L. A Popular Survey of the Old Testament. Grand Rapids, Michigan: Baker Book House Company, 1977.

Graves, Morris Jr. Faith Is A Spirit (not published or copy written).

Hagin, Kenneth E. Bible Faith Study Course. Tulsa, Oklahoma: RHEMA Bible Church, aka Kenneth Hagin Ministries, Inc., 2002.

Hagin, Kenneth E. Foundations for Faith. Tulsa, Oklahoma: RHEMA Bible Church, aka Kenneth Hagin Ministries, Inc., 1998.

Hagin, Kenneth E. Mountain Moving Faith. Tulsa, Oklahoma: RHEMA Bible Church, aka Kenneth Hagin Ministries, Inc., 2002.

Hayes, Norvel. How To Protect Your Faith. Kingwood, Texas: Hunter Books, 1978.

Hickey, Marilyn. WOW FAITH. Denver, Colorado: Legacy Publishers International, 1987.

Ortberg, John. If You Want to Walk on Water, You've Got to Get Out of the Boat. Grand Rapids, Michigan: Zondervan Inc., 2001.

Price, Frederick K.C. <u>Faith, Foolishness or Presumption?</u> Tulsa, Oklahoma: Harrison House, Inc., 1979.

Price, Frederick K.C. <u>Five Little Foxes of Faith</u>. Los Angeles, California: Faith One Publishing, 1996.

Price, Frederick K.C. <u>How to Obtain Strong Faith</u>. Los Angeles, California: Faith One Publishing, 1980.

Prince, Derek. <u>Faith To Live By</u>. New Kensington, Pennsylvania: Whitaker House, 1977.

Sanders, J. Oswald. <u>Mighty Faith</u>. Chicago, Illinois: The Moody Bible Institute of Chicago, 1971.

Simpson, A.B. <u>In the School of Faith</u>. Harrisburg, Pennsylvania: Christian Publications Inc., 1974.

<u>The King James Study Bible</u>. Nashville, Tennessee: Thomas Nelson Publishers, 1988.

<u>The NIV Matthew Henry Commentary in One Volume</u>. Grand Rapids, Michigan: Zondervan Publishing House, 1992

<u>The Oxford Pocket Dictionary and Thesaurus.</u> Oxford University Press, Inc., 1977.

<u>The Reese Chronological Bible</u>. Bloomington, Minnesota: Bethany House Publishers, 1977.

Wigglesworth, Smith. <u>Faith That Prevails</u>. Springfield, Mo: Gospel Publishing House, 1991.

Wigglesworth, Smith. <u>Smith Wigglesworth On Faith</u>. New Kensington, Pennsylvania: Whitaker House, 1998.

Webster's New World Dictionary and Thesaurus. New York, New York: Hungry Minds, Inc., 2002.

Unless otherwise noted, all scripture quotations are from the King James Version of the Bible.

Scripture references marked AMP are taken from THE COMPARATIVE STUDY BIBLE, AMPLIFIED VERSION. Copyright © 1987 by the Zondervan Corporation and the Lockman Foundation.

Scripture references marked NAS are taken from THE COMPARATIVE STUDY BIBLE, NEW AMERICAN STANDARD VERSION. Copyright © 1971, 1973, 1975, 1991, 1995 by The Lockman Foundation. All rights reserved.

Scripture references marked MSG are taken from The Message: The Bible in Contemporary Language. Copyright © 2002 by NavPress.

The International Standard Bible Encyclopedia www.studylight.org/enc/lsb/view.cgi?number=T8160>.1915. Orr, James, M.A., DD General Editor.

www.ingramcontent.com/pod-product-compliance
Lightning Source LLC
LaVergne TN
LVHW051501070426
835507LV00022B/2866